'Travellers in Faith' or 'Stealthy Legions'

About the Author

Worku Hailemariam Mohammed was born in 1962 in Addis Ababa, grew up in an Orthodox Christian family until the end of his high school years and in 1980 converted to Protestant evangelical Christianity. His mother, Jämanäšï, was born in Addis Ababa. Her mother was an Orthodox Christian and her father was a Muslim who later converted to Christianity. On his father's side, Worku's grandparents also had a mixed Orthodox-Muslim marriage and his father, brought up as a Muslim, converted to Christianity after marrying Worku's mother.

Worku trained as a cartography technician and is now a theologian who teaches Islamic courses and Qur'ānic Arabic at theological colleges in Addis Ababa where he lives. He is married with three sons and one granddaughter.

‘Travellers in Faith’ or ‘Stealthy Legions’

The Gurāgē Role in the Rise of Tablīghī Jamāʿat in Ethiopia

Worku Hailemariam Mohammed

regnum

First published 2024 by Regnum Books International

This book is an abridged version of the author's PhD thesis, ethnographic research which deals with the Tablīghī Jamā'at, an Islamic preaching movement in Ethiopia.

Regnum is an imprint of the Oxford Centre for Mission Studies
St. Philip and St. James Church
Woodstock Road, Oxford OX2 6HR, UK
www.regnumbooks.net

British Library Cataloguing in Publication Data. A catalogue record for this book is available from the British Library.

ISBN: 979-8-8898-3893-7

eBook ISBN: 979-8-8898-3894-4

Typeset in Candara by Words by Design.

Photo by Milad Fajurian www.unsplash.com

The publication of this volume is made possible through the financial assistance of Evangelisches Missionswerk.

Distributed by Fortress Press in the US, Canada, India, and Brazil

Dedication

This research is dedicated to a very important woman in my life who left a legacy of what resilience means in living for faith.

In loving memory of my late mother

Jämanäšï Gebremichael Mukhtar (1924–1998)

Tablīghīs on the move

Contents

Glossary of Terms

Arabic (Ar.), Amharic (Amh.), Gurāgē (Gur.), Oromo (Or.), Hindi (Hi.), Urdu (Ur.)

'ābid (Ar.) – one who performs much *'ibāda* or worship.

'aqīda (Ar.) – creed, belief or tenet of faith firmly based on how things are, distinct from the testimony of faith (*shahaāda*).

adab/adäbï (Ar. / Amh.) – etiquette of manner.

adab mashūra (Ar.) – etiquette of a meeting.

adab naum (Ar.) – etiquette of sleeping.

adab ta'am (Ar.) – etiquette of eating.

'adl (Ar.) – justice, fairness, equitableness, the mean between excess and falling short

aḥbab (Ar.) – love / brothers.

aḥwāl (Ar.) – progress report, condition.

'ajnabi (Ar.) – foreign / not allowed to see.

ākhira (Ar.) – the hereafter, the next world.

akhlāq (Ar.) – ethics.

'ālim (Ar.) – a man of knowledge, a scholar, especially in the sciences of Islam.

alkhalq (Ar.) – the Creator.

ajr (Ar.) – remuneration.

a'māl/ amälï (Ar. / Amh.) – virtue, character.

amarïña (Amh.) – Amharic language.

aräbïña (Amh.) – Arabic language.

Arsh (Ar.) – the Throne. It is the ceiling of all creatures and the greatest of them. The Throne contains immense expanses, height and resplendent beauty, but it is beyond the power of any human being to describe it or imagine its form. Knowledge of it is with Allāh alone. The light of the Throne is from the Light of the Noble Face of Allāh. The Throne has bearers who carry it and Allāh Almighty is settled on it, in a way that is beyond definition or concept.

asbāb/asïbabï (Ar. / Amh.) – plural of *sabab*, cause, means of obtaining something. Financial contribution for joining a *da'wa* trip.

'aṣr (Ar.) – obligatory afternoon prayer.

ayïdärïsïmï (Amh.) – not reach / get.

aye (Ur.) – is.

badrī (Ar.) – someone who took part in the battle of Badr.

balā/ bälaï (Ar. / Amh.) – calamities, catastrophes.

badliya (Ar.) – beginning.

bano (Hi.) – be.

bäqäräwï (Amh.) – the rest.

barakah/bäräka (Ar. / Amh.) – blessing.

barākallāh fīk (Ar.) – may the blessings of Allāh be upon you.

bätarikï (Amh.) – in the history.

bayān (Ar.) – clarification, elucidation: either of the substance of a meaning in the Qur'ān or of the meaning of that substance.

bida (Ar.) – innovation.

bitdaruj (Ar.) – little by little, gradually.

božä (Gur.) – god of lightning.

däjafï (Amh.) – gate.

dämwamitï (Gur.) – the deity concerned with the health and well-being of the Gurāgē.

dā'ī (Ar.) – a preacher, the one who does *da'wa,* a caller, *Tablīghī* adherent.

da'wa (Ar.) – a call to Islam.

dalīl (Ar.) – proof, indication, evidence; also a guide to Muslim homes.

deen (Ar.) – the life transaction between the Creator and created.

dhākir (Ar.) – a person who remembers / mentions the name of Allāh.

dhikr (Ar.) – lit. remembrance / mention. Commonly used, it means invocation of Allāh by repetition of His names or particular formulae. Forms include: *dhikr al-lisān, dhikr* with the tongue; *dhikr an-nafs,* recollection of the self which is inward and not audible; *dhikr al qalb,* the contemplation of the heart; *dhikr ar-rūh, dhikr* with the spirit; *dhikr as-sirr, dhikr* of the inner secret; *dhikr al-khafī,* secret recollection; *dhikr akhfā al-khafī,* the most secret remembrance of the secret.

Dīn al Islām (Ar.) – Islamic faith.

du'ā' (Ar.) – prayer, making supplication to Allāh.

dunyā (Ar.) – secular / worldly, not as a cosmic phenomenon but as imagined and experienced.

fāiṣala (Ar.) – say.

falāḥ (Ar.) – success, prosperity, the lasting attainment of that which one desires.

fanonätï (Gur.) – migration to urban area, mainly economic migrant.

fanonätï (Amh.) – migration to the bush, mainly political migrant.

fano (Gur.) – a person who migrates to another area, mainly for economic reasons.

fano (Amh.) – young combatant who migrates to the bush, mainly for war.

faqīh (Ar.) – a man learned in the knowledge of *fiqh* who, by virtue of his knowledge, can give a legal judgement.

farḍ (Ar.) – obligatory, an obligatory act of worship or practice of the *Dīn* as defined by the *Sharī'a*.

fāsid (Ar.) – irregular, invalid, corrupt.

fi-sabilillah (Ar.) – in the way of Allāh.

fatwā (Ar.) – an authoritative statement on a point of law.

fitna (Ar.) – temptation.

fikr/fikrā (Ar.) – reflection, seeking the meaning of things as manifestations of the Divine. Also *tafakkur* .

fiqh (Ar.) – the science of the application of the *sharī'a*. A practitioner or expert in *fiqh* is called *faqīh*

gatā (Or.) – tomb.

gaflah of *iman/gäfila* (Ar. / Amh.) – depressed of faith, depression.

gweyïtakwe (Gur.) – honourable.

Häbäša or *Habāsha* (Amh. / Ar.) – Abyssinian Ethiopian highlanders or Ethiopians and those of East, West and some parts of Central Africa.

Ḥadīth (Ar.) – reported speech of the Prophet Muḥammad.

ḥāfiz (Ar.) – someone who has memorised the Qur'ān.

Hajj (Ar.) – the annual pilgrimage to Mekkah, which is one of the five pillars of Islam.

ḥalāl (Ar.) – lawful in the *sharī'a.*

ḥalaqa (Ar. / Ur.) – a circle of people gathered for the purpose of study.

ḥarārm (Ar.) – unlawful in the *sharī'a.*

ḥaqq/haqï (Ar. / Amh.) – the Real, the Absolute Truth, Allāh, being the opposite of *Khāliq*, creation. Rights and justice.

hay (Ar.) – live.

ḥayāt (Ar.) – life.

hayātu ṣaḥāba (Ar.) – lives of the Companions of Muḥammad.

ḥidāya (Ar.) – guidance, active guidance from Allāh, debriefing.

hifiz (Ar.) – memorisation.

ḥikma (Ar.) – wisdom.

hirasa (Ar.) – guard.

'ibāda (Ar.) – act of worship.

ïdïme (Amh.) – age.

ikhlāṣ (Ar.) – sincerity, pure unadulterated genuineness.

ikhlāṣ niyya (Ar.) – loyalty and intention.

ikhtilaf (Ar.) – controversial questions, juristic disagreement.

ikhtilam (Ar.) – wet dream.

ikrām (Ar.) – gift.

ikramel muslim (Ar.) – respect to all Muslims, including all creatures.

'ilm (Ar.) – knowledge, science.

'ilm and *dhikr* (Ar.) – knowledge and remembrance.

imām (Ar.) – Muslim religious or political leader, head of the mosque.

īmān/ (Ar./Amh.) – belief, faith, acceptance of Allāh and His Messenger. Belief consists of believing in Allāh, His angels, His Books, His Messengers, the Last Day, the Garden of Fire and that everything, both good and bad, is by the decree of Allāh.

inḟirād (Ar.) – solitude.

ingilizignā (Amh.) – English language.

'ishā' (Ar.) – obligatory evening prayer.

ishrāf (Ar.) – covet.

ïsïkä (Amh.) – until.

islaah (Ar.) – reformation.

isrāf (Ar.) – profusion.

istighfār (Ar.) – to ask the forgiveness of Allāh, especially by saying, '*Astagfiru' llāh*' ('I seek the forgiveness of Allāh').

istinjā (Ar.) – washing the private parts with water.

istiqāma (Ar.) – integrity and straightness/rectitude, rightness.

istiqbāl (Ar.) – the team in charge of reception.

jahannam/jähanamï (Ar./Amh.) – Hell, *Gehenna*.

jalla jalālhu (Ar.) – the formula said after the name of Allāh meaning great is His Majesty.

jamā'a/ jäma (Ar./Amh.) – the main body of Muslim community; also designates the group prayer, team.

jamā'at (Ar.) – team.

jam' (Ar.) – gatheredness, combining all into the whole and ignoring structures in existence in an undifferentiated field of awareness by witnessing Allah.

Jämanäši (Amh. / Ar.) – you are many, a meaning of my mother's name.

janna (Ar.) – the garden, heaven, paradise.

jaula (Ar.) – going around doing *da'wa.*

jihād (Ar.) – struggle, particularly fighting in the way of Allāh to establish Islam.

jihūd (Ar.) – struggle.

jumu'a (Ar.) – the day of gathering, Friday, and particularly the *Jumu'a,* prayer which is performed instead of ẓuhr by those who attend it. Friday only acquired this name with the coming of Islam. Before that it was known as *al-'Arūba.*

ka'ba (Ar.) – the cube-shaped building at the centre of the haram in Makka, originally built by the Prophet Ibrāhīm. Also known as the House of Allāh. It is towards *Ka'ba* that Muslims face when praying.

kāfir (Ar.) – a person who rejects Allāh and His Messenger.

kälelä (Amh.) – if not there.

kalīma toyba (Ar.) – the first virtue of Tablīghīs and main article of faith, there is no god but Allāh.

karāmā (Ar.) – miracles, nobility, dignity.

khāliq (Ar.) – 'creature,' both the act of creation or the result of the act, hence the cosmos.

khalwa/hälawa (Ar. / Gur.) – spiritual retreat, seclusion, in order to remember Allāh; traditionally, it was considered as a little grass hut built in the main compound of Abret, recently changed to little tin-roofed huts.

khārijites (Ar.) – or *khawārij,* the earliest sect that separated themselves from the body of the Muslims and declared war on all those who disagreed with them, stating a wrong action turns a Muslim into an unbeliever.

khat/ č'atï (Amh.) – a leafy stimulant for mild intoxication, it is commonly grown in the Gurāgē area, the eastern part of Ethiopia, and also Yemen and Kenya. It is a popular drug among Muslim communities in general, and in the Gurāgē community in particular. It is also called *miraa* in Kiswahili.

khayr (Ar.) – good.

khāzin/ (Ar.) – a treasurer, storekeeper, guard.

khidma/ mäkadämï (Ar. / Amh.) – treating others, cooking and the like.

khilaf (Ar.) – differences in Islamic jurisprudence.

khmasmal (Ar.) – five main works.

khurūj fi-sabililah (Ar.) – going out in the way of Allāh.

Kitāb (Ar. / Or.) – book.

la 'ilāha'illla-llāh muḥammadun rasūlu llāh (Ar.) – there is no deity except Allāh, and Muḥammad is the Messenger of Allāh.

lāmāqāmi māsāweq/ lämäqami masawäqï (Ar. / Amh.) – informing to the area head. (A combination of Amharic and Arabic.)

lamazayr/ lämäzäyärï (Ar. / Amh.) – to visit. (A combination of Amharic and Arabic.)

läsïntï gize näwï yämiwät'awï ? (Amh.) – for how long are you going out?

Laylat al-Qadr (Ar.) – the Night of Power, mentioned in *Sūrah* 97 of the Qur'ān

maïkälï (Amh.) – centre.

maghrib (Ar.) – obligatory evening prayer.

malfoozaat (Ar. / Ur.) – sound words / attractions.

maqāmi (Ar.) – site, part of *khmasmal,* which takes place on Sundays.

maqbūd (Ar.) – held / grasped.

maqṣid (Ar.) – intention, goal, end, objective.

marakiz (Ar.) – centre, *khuruj* to India, Pakistan and Bangladesh.

mashāikh (Ar.) – greybeard.

māshā'llāh (Ar.) – interesting, wonderful, expressing joyful feelings.

mashūra (Ar.) – consulting with experts, consultative group, meeting and council.

masjid/mäsïgidï (Ar. / Amh.) – mosque.

masturat (Ar.) – spousal preaching team, women *khuruj/da'wa.*

masul (Ar.) – leader.

mawlānā (Ur.) – senior man and master.

mawlid (Ar.) – birth day of the Prophet Muhammad.

mayyit (Ar.) – dead.

mazhabs (Ar.) – schools of thought.

mätawäqiya (Amh.) – identity card (ID).

mïdïbï (Amh.) – group.

minda/mïnïda (Ar. / Amh.) – income, salary / blessing.

mïnïtafi (Amh.) – carpet.

miskin/mïsïkinï (Ar. / Amh.) – poor, polite.

mote (Amh.) – my death.

muballighin (Ar.) – a person who participates in Tablīgh.

muhaba (Ar.) – love.

mu'min/mïïmänï (Ar. / Amh.) – a believer, someone who possesses *īmān*, who trusts in Allāh.

muraqaba (Ar.) – vigilance; recollection; an aspect of reflection (*tafakkur*); waiting on a spiritual presence; permanent state of awareness rather than a spiritual exercise; Sufi meditation.

murid (Ar.) – disciple. He is the one who is stripped of his will (*irāda*) and hands himself over to his shaykh, his guide.

murshid (Ar.) – a spiritual guide.

musfāir (Ar.) – traveller, one who travels with his intellect through intelligible matters.

musleman (Ur. / Hi.) – Muslim.

muṣallā (Ar.) – a place for praying.*'Id* prayers are normally held outside the mosque at *muṣallā*; the term is sometimes used for a prayer mat.

mustaid (Ar.) – prepared for a specific task.

mutakallim (Ar.) – someone who studies the science of *kalām*, the science of investigating and articulating religious belief; (spokesman of the team at *jaula*).

muta hijab (Ar.) – veiling women.

mutqalba (Ar.) – changeful.

nafīla (Ar.) – supererogatory or voluntary act of worship.

nafsiya/näfäsï (Ar. / Amh.) – soul, ego.

najāḥ (Ar.) – success.

näwïrï (Amh.) – shame.

nii'ma (Ar.) – grace.

niqbāb (Ar.) – veil which covers the entire face, including eyes.

niyya (Ar.) – intention.

nūr (Ar.) – light.

panchāyat (Hi.) – a traditional meeting of the elders in a village / jury.

qābliya (Ar.) – capability.

qadīm/qädami (Ar. / Amh.) – eternal, ancient, elderly; a person who has been around for a long time.

qalb/qälïbï (Ar. / Amh.) – heart; the faculty for directly perceiving spiritual realities that the mind cannot grasp.

qänï/qänočï (Amh.) – day / days.

qaylula (Ar.) – power nap, straight after lunch.

qiṣṣa (Ar.) – a popular story, connected narrative or piece of propaganda.

qiyāma (Ar.) – the arising of people at the Resurrection on the Last Day.

quwanïqwa (Amh.) – language.

radiya'llahu 'anhu (Ar.) – may Allāh be pleased with him.

radiya'llahu 'anhā (Ar.) – may Allāh be pleased with her.

radiya'llahu 'anhum (Ar.) – may Allāh be pleased with them.

raḥmat (Ar.) – mercy.

rak'a(t) (Ar.) – a unit of prayer consisting of a series of standings, bowings, prostrations and sittings.

ramaḍān (Ar.) – fasting month.

ribā (Ar.) – usury, which is *ḥarārm,* whatever forms it takes, since it involves obtaining something for nothing through exploitation.

riyā (Ar.) – showing off, doing actions for the sake of being seen to do them.

rizq/rïzïqï (Ar. / Amh.) – rations issued to soldiers, provisions, daily bread.

rūh/ruhï (Ar. / Amh.) – the soul, vital spirit.

sabab/säbabï (Ar. / Amh.) – cause, means of obtaining something.

ṣabr (Ar.) – patience.

ṣadaqa/sädäqa (Ar. / Amh.) – charitable giving in the Cause of Allāh, feast to feed people.

ṣaḥāba (Ar.) – the Companion of the Prophet Muḥammad; may Allāh bless him and grant him peace. If a Muslim has seen the Prophet, or talked to him at least once when the Prophet was alive, he is called *ṣaḥābī*. The plural form of *ṣaḥābī is ṣaḥāba* or *Aṣḥāb*. The word *ṣaḥāba al-Kirām* includes all of those great people, each of whom has seen the Prophet at least once.

sahih (Ar.) – true, correct, reliable.

sallā'llāhu 'alayhi wa sallam (Ar.) – 'may Allāh bless him and grant him peace.' The formula spoken after mentioning the Prophet Muḥammad.

ṣalāt (Ar.) – the prayer, particularly the five daily obligatory prayers. One of the five pillars of Islam.

säwï (Amh.) – human.

säwočï (Amh.) – people.

sayïramädu (Amh.) – without walking.

sayyidi (Ar.) – a descendant of the Prophet; also master.

sayyidinā (Ar.) – our respected master.

shafā'a (Ar.) – intercession, particularly the intercession of the Prophet Muḥammad on the Last Day.

shahaāda (Ar.) – bearing witness, particularly bearing witness that there is no god but Allāh and that Muḥammad is the Messenger of Allāh. It is one of the pillars of Islam. It is used for legal testimony in a court of law. It also means martyrdom.

shahīd (Ar.) – martyr who dies fighting in the Cause of Allāh.

shāhid (Ar.) – a witness, another narration that supports the meaning of a *ḥadīth* which is being investigated with an entirely different *isnād*.

shar/šärï (Ar. / Amh.) – evil.

sharḥ (Ar.) – commentary.

shayṭān/säyïtanï (Ar. / Amh.) – a devil, particularly *Iblīs*, one of the *jinn*.

sharī'a (Ar.) – literally road, the legal modality of a people based on the Revelation of their Prophet. The final *sharī'a* is that of Islam.

shirk/šärïkï (Ar. / Amh.) – partnering Allāh with something, partnership.

shukr/šukurï (Ar. / Gur.) – thanksgiving.

shūrā (Ar.) – consultation, a council.

ṣifa (Ar.) – attribute.

silsila (Ar.) – the chain, in Sufism, the continuity of spiritual descent and transmission of wisdom from *shaykh* to *shaykh* from the Prophet.

ṣifatu sitta (Ar.) – the six points / virtues / principles of the Tablīghī Jamā'at.

siyāsa/siyasa (Ar. / Or.) – rule, governance, as contrasted with divine *sharī'a*, political talk.

subhān wa ta'ala (Ar.) – Glorified He is exalted.

subhi (Ar.) – morning obligatory prayer.

sūrah (Ar.) – chapter of the Qur'ān. The Qur'ān is composed of 114 *sūrahs*.

sujūd (Ar.) – prostration.

sunna (Ar.) – the customary practice of a person or group of people. It has come to refer almost exclusively to the practice of the Messenger of Allāh and to the first generation of Muslims.

sunnī (Ar.) – the main body of Muslims, the *Ahl as Sunna wa'l-Jamā'a,* who recognise and accept the *Khulafā' ar-Rāshidūn,* the first four khalifs.

tablīgh (Ar. /Ur.) – to convey, to reach a message.

Tablīghī Jamā'at (Ar./Ur.) – a preaching party, currently known as one of an Islamic religious movement.

Tābi'un/tābi'uoch (Ar./Amh.) – members of post-*ṣaḥāba* generation. (Combined with Amharic.)

tafakkur (Ar.) – pondering, reflection.

ta'līm (Ar.) – study group, seeking knowledge.

tafrigh (Ar.) – spare time.

takfīr (Ar.) – to declare that someone is a *kafīr*. A practice introduced by the *Khārijites.*

takwīn/täkänawänä (Ar./Amh.) – bringing into being.

tamīr al-masjid (Ur.) – a group of individuals who are willing to stay at a mosque and give guidance (*ḥidāya*) and support to those who arrive at the mosque.

täqädami (Amh.) – prior.

tāqarābu/täqaräbu (Ar./Amh.) – come nearer.

taqwā (Ar.) – awe or fear of Allāh, which inspires a person to be on guard against wrong action and eager for actions that please Him.

tära-qut'ïrï (Amh.) – serial number.

targhib (Ar.) – motivational talk.

tariqa-i-Tablīgh (Ar.) – the method of preaching.

tartīb/tärïtibï (Ar. / Or.) – proper sequence of actions in the prayer, *wuḍū'*, *ḥajj* or scheduling.

tashahhud (Ar.) – literally to make *shahaāda*. In the context of the prayer, it is a formula which includes the *shahaāda* and is said in the final sitting position of each of two rak'at cycles. Sitting style at a study group.

tasbīḥ (Ar.) – glorification, saying '*Subḥān Allāh,*' 'Glory to Allāh'; prayer beads.

tashībh (Ar.) – anthropomorphism, comparing Allāh to created things or making Allāh resemble created things. Opposite of *tanzīh*.

tanzīh (Ar.) – transcendence, disconnecting Allāh from creation.

tawba (Ar.) – turning away from wrong action; instead, turning towards Allāh and asking His forgiveness.

tawfiq (Ar.) – success given by Allāh.

tawajihu (Ar.) – direction / orientation.

tawakaltu (Ar.) – puts one's trust in Allāh.

tijaniyya (Ar.) – *tariqa* in the Maghrib founded by Abu'l-'Abbas Ahmad at-Tijani (d. 1230 / 1815) in Fes. They are exclusivist, not allowing people to join any other *tariqa,* and advocate complete submission to the government, whatever it is.

'ulamā' / ulāma (Ar. / Amh.) – scholars, scholar.

'ulamā ziyāra/ulāma ziyara (Ar. / Amh.) – visiting religious leaders / scholar.

umma (Ar.) – the body of Muslims as one distinct community.

ummat/ (Ar. / Or.) – Muslim community, people.

umumi ziyara (Ar.) – public visit, home-to-home visit.

ususi ziyara (Ar.) – selected home-to-home visit.

usul (Ar.) – origins.

walī (Ar.) – someone who is a 'friend' of Allāh, thus possessing the quality of *wilāya.*

wärï (Amh.) – month.

waswas/wäsïwasï (Ar. / Amh.) – scruple.

wuḍū' (Ar.) – ritual washing with water to be pure for the prayer of hands, mouth, nostrils, face, forearms, head, ears and feet.

yäfïtu (Amh.) – future.

yähwalawï (Amh.) – past.

yā jamā'a/ya jäma (Ar. / Amh.) – code of the team.

yākhārijin/yäharijinï sïmï-zïrïzïrï (Ar. / Amh.) – list of names of a team member.

yälämï (Amh.) – no.

ya llāh musfāir/yälahï musafirï (Ar. / Amh.) – Allāh's traveller.

yamāsjid/yämasjidu sïmï (Ar. / Amh.) – the name of the mosque.

yä-mimäläsubätï qänï (Amh.) – date of return.

yanažä täbärašä (Gur.) – who doesn't see Abret, spoiled.

yä qänï yākhārijin/yäharijinï jämaï mäkäwäňa forïmï (Ar. / Amh.) – the actual date of implementation of the traveller.

yaqīn (Ar.) – absolute unshakeable certainty and certitude.

yā-tashkil bota (Ar. / Amh.) – place, where the trip will be.

yä -wät'ubätï qänï (Amh.) – date of going out.

Yawm al-Qiyāma (Ar.) – 'the Day of Rising,' the Day of Standing.

yä mät'ubülubutï katama (Amh.) – town of origin.

yäzarenï (Amh.) – today (currently).

yraḥimahu'llāh (Ar.) – may Allāh have mercy on him.

zawīya (Ar.) – a 'corner,' small mosque, or religious retreat, often where the *shaykh* teaches.

zina (Ar.) – adultery.

ziyāra/ *ziyara* (Ar./Amh.) – visit to tomb or holy places, visiting homes and people.

ẓuhr (Ar.) – noon obligatory prayer.

Introduction

This mini-book is based on the author's PhD thesis, ethnographic research which deals with the Tablīghī Jamā'at, an Islamic preaching movement in Ethiopia. The thesis generated primary sources through live participant observation, oral history, interviews and country visits, including India where the movement began. The thesis argues that even though it is a transnational movement, Tablīghī Jamā'at in Ethiopia manifests local identity and also maintains global connections.

Exploring Tablīghī Jamā'at

Introduction

Tablīghī Jamā'at is one of the largest lay religious movements in the world whose primary objective is the renewal of Islam around the world. From its rise in a rural setting in India to its global spread in less than a decade, Tablīghī Jamā'at illustrates a significant variety of Muslim transnationalism that focuses on the renewal of Muslims and *da'wa* (proselytising). Despite its worldwide influence on the lives of millions of Muslims, scholars have paid almost no attention to its spreading in Ethiopia and Sub-Saharan Africa.

This book, a precis of the author's PhD thesis, explores the nature of the Gurāgē affiliation with Tablīghī Jamā'at and the role this alliance plays in the growth of Sunni Islam in Ethiopia. It also contributes to the extent to which local ethnic, religious and political interrelations and conflicts are contributing to the transformation of Islam in Ethiopia.

Ethiopia is located in the Horn of Africa and has been a home for Christians and Muslims for over a thousand years. Traditionally,

Ethiopia has been considered a Christian island but since the 7th century, Islam has been practised by millions of people. The 2007 census shows that while Christians accounted for 63% (Orthodox 43%, Protestant 19%, Catholic 1%), Muslims accounted for 34%, and the remaining 3% belonged to different indigenous traditions.

Ethiopia is a country with a population of 119 million of whom 21% live in cities. It is administratively divided into 11 Regions and two Chartered Cities, each having its own governance. The Regions are divided according to ethnic and linguistic identity. The median age in Ethiopia is 19 and it is a country with over 88 ethnic and language groups of varying sizes from the smallest, Qewama (about 500), to the average, Gurāgē (five million), and the largest, Oromo (about 40 million).

Ethiopia is also considered a home for African countries for several reasons. Firstly, Addis Ababa is Africa's diplomatic capital where the Organisation of African Unity (later named the African Union) established itself in 1963 with 32 heads of independent African states signing the charter. Currently, the African Union consists of 55 member states that make up the countries of the African continent. Secondly, Ethiopia has never been colonised and serves as an example of freedom for Africa. Thirdly, African leaders consider Ethiopia as their mother. In October 2021 when the Ethiopian Prime Minister, Dr Abiy Ahmed Ali, was sworn in for a new five-year term, the Kenyan and South Sudanese Presidents, in their congratulatory speeches, addressed Ethiopia as their mother.

Ethiopia has often been described as a 'Christian nation' because of the importance of the Ethiopian Orthodox (Täwahïdo) Church and its connection with the power structure since the 4th century. The late Emperors King Menelik and Häyïläsïlase (1889–1913; 1930–1974) claimed that Ethiopia is a Christian island, and the state and Christianity are the two faces of a coin. That notion has been challenged because Ethiopia (the Axumite Empire) became a home for the refugees *Ṣaḥāba* (the Companions of the Prophet Muḥammad) in the year 615. This was after they were persecuted by the Quraysh authorities in Mecca. The Prophet Muḥammad told his followers: "If you go to Abyssinia you will find a king under whom none are persecuted. It is a land of righteousness where God will give you relief from your suffering."

Islam in Ethiopia

Bilal bin Rabah al Habäshi is identified as the first Ethiopian *mu'adhdhin* (a caller to prayer) and Gurāgē convert. Nevertheless, Islam was not adopted widely as a religion for the Gurāgē people until the 12th century. At the beginning of the 16th century, Islam and Christianity were both introduced by Ahmad Ibn Ibrahim al-Ghazi (1506–1543, nicknamed Ahmad *Gragn,* meaning the left-handed) and the Abyssinian King Galawdios. Both used forced conversion of the Gurāgē people to Islam or Christianity. Before Islam, indigenous traditions and beliefs were deeply rooted in the Gurāgē culture. During the 16th to 18th centuries, the Gurāgēs religion was called 'belief of *bože* (god of lightning)', which identified the firstborn of the cultural worship leader as the next leader in the chain. This chain contained seven generations of leaders under the title of *goŷtakuya* (honourable). In the 1850s, after Niqye *goŷtakuya,* his son, Sayid Ibrahim, broke this line of worship and accepted Islam through a dream and went to Geto Woreda, Yeqonet Sheikh and Sheikh Yusuf to have Islamic religious teachings.

When Sayid Ibrahim's first son, Sayid Bushra, was born in 1878 in the western part of Gurāgē, he continued Islamic practices, not only following his father in Islamic traditions but establishing Abret as an Islamic teaching centre and a place of worship, and became the first Abret Sheikh.

Consequently, since the lifetime of the Prophet Muḥammad, Ethiopia has had a special place in the history of Islam. However, Orthodox Ethiopian leaders have suppressed Islam, considering it an alien religion. This suppression had a strong impact on the lives of the Ethiopian Muslims which led them to struggle for their freedom and equality. In April 1974, a demonstration in Addis Ababa led Muslims, to protest the joint single religious mission of the state and its benefactor, the Ethiopian Orthodox Täwahïdo Church. Until the 1974 socio-political revolution in Ethiopia, the Ethiopian Orthodox Täwahïdo Church was considered the state religion. But since 1974, a new political system has arisen under the name of '*yator hailoch astabbabari darg*' (a coordination committee of military force), which introduced a Communist ideology to the country. The 1974 socio-political revolution overthrew the feudal elites. From then on, the state and religion were separate entities.

Unlike other regimes, the 1995 Ethiopian Constitution realised that the state could not interfere in religious affairs and vice versa. The Ethiopian People's Revolutionary Democratic Front, which has been instrumental in drafting the new constitution, introduced a much more flexible policy to secure the rights, freedom and equality of ethnic and religious communities.

The longstanding request for recognition of Ethiopian Muslims was addressed by the Ethiopian government following a proclamation of the Council of the House of Representatives on 4 July 2020. This provided legality for the Ethiopian Islamic Affairs General Council. This automatically put Islam on the same standing as the Ethiopian Orthodox Täwahïdo Church, which operates without annual or biannual registration. Evangelical Christians likewise obtained the same legal status with the name 'Ethiopian Council of Gospel Believers, Churches and Members' on the same day. Such proclamations will provide more freedom of expression for Muslims and Christians.

The **Tablīghī Jamā'at** is a 20th-century Islamic faith renewal movement whose adherents claim that they are imitating the footsteps of the early days of Prophet Muḥammad's Companions through their *da'wa* (proselytising) practice. While previous studies of Tablīghī Jamā'at have included India, South Asia, Australia, Kenya and Gambia, little attention has been given to Ethiopia.

There are two views by scholars who study Tablīghī Jamā'at. Many scholars view Tablīghī Jamā'at as 'travellers in faith' and argue that "Tablīghī Jamā'at exists mainly to focus on the renewal

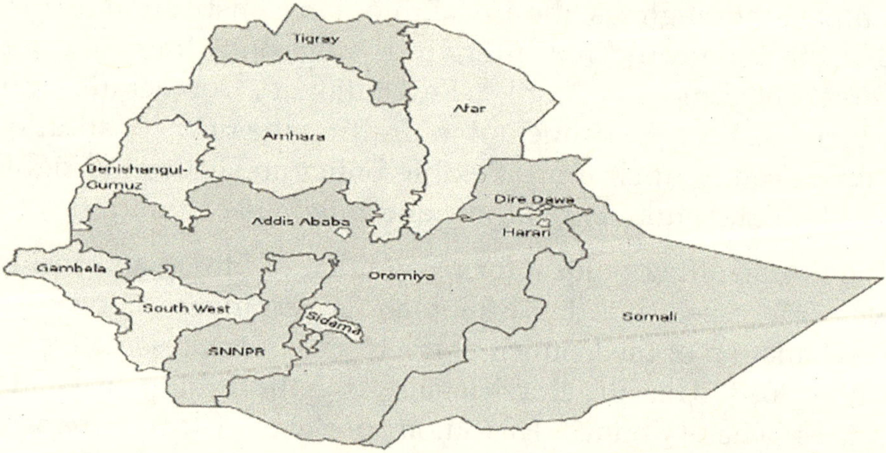

Ethiopia: Map of 11 Regional States and Two Chartered Cities

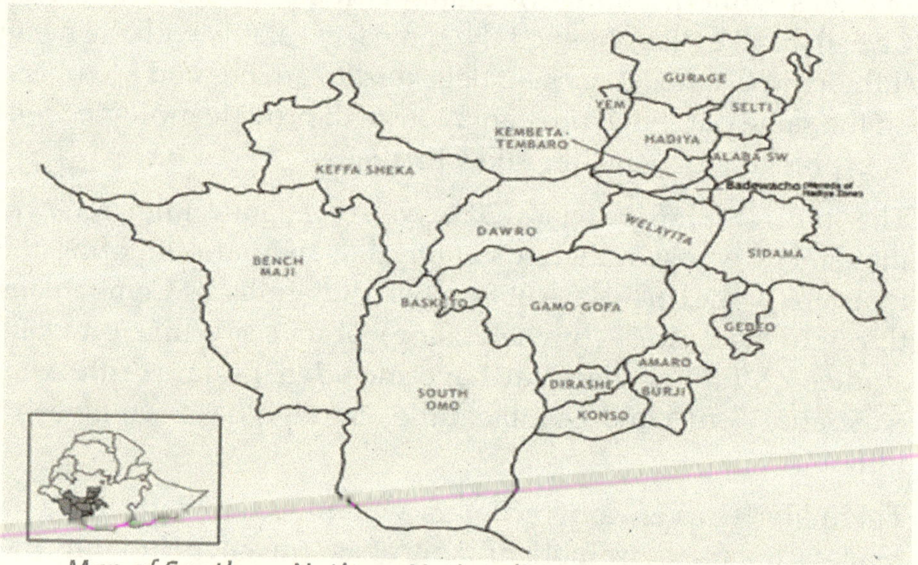

Map of Southern Nations, Nationalities and Peoples' Region

of Muslims and *da'wa*" and suggest that the purpose of founding Tablīghī Jamā'at was for the promotion and preservation of Islamic identity and faith. However, a few scholars view Tablīghī Jamā'at as 'stealthy legions,' suggesting Tablīghī Jama'at's actions and motives have grave implications for promoting the war on terrorism.

The Origin of Tablīghī Jamā'at in India

The word Tablīghī Jamā'at comes from two Arabic words: *tablīgh* – 'to reach the message' or 'propagation of the message of Islam,' and *jamā'a* – 'the main body of the Muslim community.' It was founded by Mawlana Muḥammad Ilyas Khandhalwi (1885–1944) in the early 1920s in Northern India for the promotion and preservation of Islamic identity and faith.

Mawlana Muḥammad Ilyas Khandhalwi was born in 1885. His childhood was spent in his maternal grandfather's home in Kandhla, with his father, Mawlana Muḥammad Ismail, at Nizamuddin. His mother had memorised the Qur'ān by heart and she was called *ḥāfizal* Qur'ān. Ilyas was her favourite child and she used to say to him, "Ilyas, I feel the aroma of the holy Companions in you."

Mawlana Muḥammad Ilyas stayed for nine years with his teacher / mentor, Mawlana Rasheed Ahmed Gangohi, and his death was the second shock for Ilyas following the death of his own father. In 1908, Ilyas undertook his theological training with Dārul 'Ulūm

Deoband,[1] one of the oldest Islamic schools in India, established in 1866, and studied Tirmizi and Sahih Bukhari from Mawlana Mahmood Hasan. Two years later he started teaching at the Madrassa of Mazaahirul Uloom and in 1912, he married his cousin.

In 1925, Ilyas went on Pilgrimage (*Hajj*) to Mecca and during this time he set apart three silent days of contemplation at the Mosque of the Prophet Muḥammad in Medina. Ilyas claimed to have accepted his call for *Tablīgh* (preaching) through the Prophet Muḥammad. He returned to India with renewed enthusiasm and a greater faith in his mission, having been 'called' in the way of the *tariqa-i-Tablīgh* (the method of preaching) and began his pioneering work in Mewat, near Delhi. Ilyās was influenced not only by the Deobandi teaching where he studied but also by the strong influence of his mother.

Ilyas started the Tablīghī Jamā'at in 1926 and his first choice for *da'wa* (missionary) tour was Kandhla, his home town and a well-known religious and educational centre for Muslims. In the month of Ramadhan, a team (*jamā'a*) of ten Mewatis (Mēwātīs) went to Kandhla. According to Masud, the purpose of this tour was to seek the support of the scholars (*'ulama*) for their ideas. The Tablīgh work expanded into the entire territory of Mewat by organising 16 *jamā'at* (teams) to do *da'wa* tours with a leader (*amir*) and a leader of leaders (*amirul umara*).

In 1934, he presented a programme of action that consisted of fifteen points at a traditional meeting of the elders in a village

[1] The **Deobandi** movement or Deobandism is a revivalist movement within Sunni Islam that adheres to the Hanafi school of law. It formed in the late 19th century.

(*panchāyat*). The meeting defined four objectives of the *da'wa*: i) universal participation of all classes of Muslims; ii) focus on action and physical movement; iii) adoption of learning, teaching, serving and promoting religion as a way of life; and iv) temporary migration from one's native place as a religious obligation. Since 1934, Tablīghī Jamā'at has become one of the largest Islamic renewal movements in the world among Sunni Muslims. As a sect, they belong to the Ahlus-Sunnah wal-Jamaah. By Madhhab they are Hanafee; in conduct, they are Sufis. Scholastically, they are *Maturidi* (mourning), and in *Sulook* (behaviour), they are Chishti. Thus, they combine all Sufi orders. And in *nisbat* (ratio), they are Deobandi.

Although Tablīghī Jamā'at has now planted many different bases around the world, it remains connected to its original South Asian roots. In 1946, the Tablīghīs sent their first delegations to England and the Arabian Hijaz, and in the late 1940s and early 1950s, the movement had extended to South Asia, Europe and North Africa. In 1956, Southern and Eastern African countries received their first Tablīghīs visits and Tablīghī Jamā'at began operating in The Gambia in the 1960s and Ethiopia in the 1970s.

It has now become one of the largest global Islamic renewal movements with a presence in about 165 countries across six continents.

The Origin of Tablīghī Jamā'at in Ethiopia

The Tablīghī Jamā'at movement came to Ethiopian soil in the 1960s and was well received by Haji Musa Mahmood Ahmad Kikiya, who was of Eritrean origin. Haji Musa is remembered as the founding father of the Tablīghī Jamā'at work in Ethiopia and he was elected as the first national *amir* (leader) at the first *mashūra* (meeting) which took place at The Grand Anwar Masjid, one of the three oldest mosques in Addis Ababa.

Haji Musa Mahmood Ahmad Kikiya was born in 1936 in Hirgigo, Massawa, Eritrea. His father was Mahmood Ahmad Kikiya and his mother was Hajiya Fatuma Haji Ahmad Kikiya. The Kikiyan family were well-known traders and Haji Musa went to a primary school in Asmara, Eritrea. He then attended secondary school and university in Addis Ababa, graduating with a BA degree in Business Administration. Following that, he worked as an officer at the Ethiopian Civilisation Office from 1955 to 1957. He was married, with two wives and eight children.

Haji Musa's family is known by the name Kikiyas. They were strong Muslims whose roots trace back to the Turkish traders who came to Eritrea when the Turks controlled the Red Sea. By the 1850s they were well-known traders in that area. Upon the Italian invasion of Ethiopia, the Kikiyans came to Ethiopia and made a significant contribution to Ethiopian trade and economy, and Haji Musa is remembered as an importer and exporter.

Haji Musa made his first Tablīgh tour to a well-known traditional Islamic religious and education centre in the heartland of the Gurāgē ethnic people at Abret, where the famous and respected Abret Sheikh, Sayyid Budala, lived. Sayid Budala's contact with Haji Musa is considered one of the historic events in Islam among the Gurāgē people. Haji Musa introduced the Tablīghī teaching to the Abret Sheikh and the people around him. Sayid Budala visited Haji Musa's mother in Addis Ababa because he heard that she was *ḥāfizal*-Qur'ān (memorised the Qur'ān) just like the mother of Sheikh Ilyas. Haji Musa had said that a Muslim should have his own sheikh, and Haji Musa considered Sayid Budala, the Abret Sheikh, as his own sheikh.

In 1976, during the period of Military Junta Regime (Derg 1974–1991) in Ethiopia, Haji Musa was arrested but released after a few weeks of imprisonment. In 1994, with the then Ethiopian government, the Ethiopian People's Revolutionary Democratic Front took Haji Musa to the Central Criminal Investigation Office, traditionally known as the Central (*maekelawi*), and interrogated him. The authorities thought that the Tablīgh movement would make the younger generation too idealistic and became suspicious of a hidden agenda within the Tablīgh movement. Haji Musa argued the benefits of *da'wa*, and stated that, unless the younger generation cultivated their lifestyle in an ethical way, according to the life transaction (*deen*) of Islam to be a good Muslim and take part in a religious tour, they would prove a serious challenge to the government with such a low employment rate. Haji Musa was finally released home peacefully.

He was also encouraging authors to write or translate books on the Tablīghī Jamā'at movement so that people could gain a deeper understanding of it. In 2002, towards the end of his life, he gave an order for a translation work on a book that would explain the six points of the Tablīghī Jamā'at movement. This book was translated into Amharic, the working language of Ethiopia, and printed in June 2013.

Haji Musa died on 6 March 2003 at the age of 67 in Addis Ababa, creating a huge gap in leadership. Only one of Haji Musa's daughters, Zaynab Haji Musa Kikiya, followed in her father's

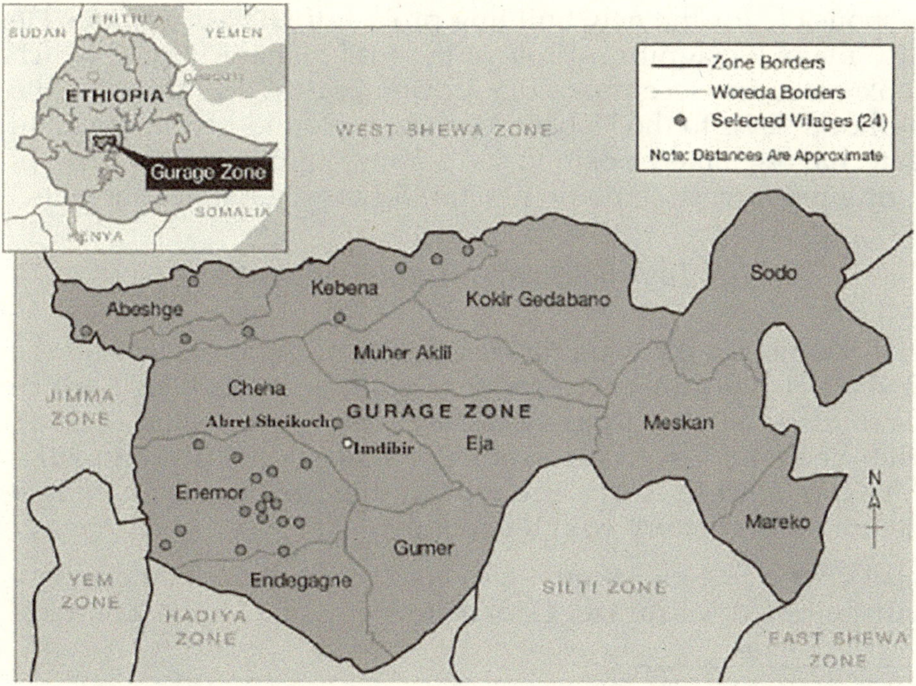

Gurāgē Zone Map Showing Abret Sheikoch with Woredas

footsteps and although all of them have remained Muslims, they have not been interested in committing themselves to the faith as their father did. One of the reasons for this is that they did not regard leaving their homes and travelling for days, weeks, or months as a parental duty.

After the death of Haji Musa, the leadership of the movement operated through the 22 elected *shūrā* (council) members and each member would become an *amir* (leader) in rotation on a monthly basis. Sheikh engineer Ali Khadir was one member, a well-educated man, committed to the Tablīghī Jamā'at, who worked tirelessly day and night for the movement and has been responsible for the new building project of Häbäša Markaz. He also played a significant role at the first Häbäša Ijtima,[2] which took place in December 2019 in Butajira town. In one of the author's visits to the Häbäša Markaz, he found him at the main gate having taken position as a *ḥirāsa* (guard). This type of humility is a very common practice for most Tablīgh adherents.

Haji Zaynu Sheikh Muqina (1923–2013)

Haji Zaynu Sheikh Muqina was the founding member and the first *imām* (Muslim congregational leader) of the mosque which he founded in 1970 (Masjid Markaz/Abubakar Asidiq Masjid), and where he served for over 40 years until his death in 2013. Muslims in Addis Ababa also call this mosque Haji Zaynu Masjid because of its history with the founder.

Haji Zaynu Sheikh Muqina was born of the Mazaraze clan in a village called Mazaraze, Gadabano Woreda, Gurāgē Zone. He

[2] Ijtima is an annual gathering which takes place where the Tablīghī Jamā'at movement is active with tens of thousands of adherents.

studied Islamic education in a traditional way, first from his mother, Ade-Nafisa, for six years and continued under well-known *sheikhs* in the Gurāgē land, Addis Ababa and Mecca.

People who knew Haji Zaynu remember him as courageous, reliable, a born *dais* (missionary), very practical and always looking for the positive aspects in everyone. He was constantly on the move to present people with a strong and attractive message of Islam and gave complete freedom for the *da'wa jamā'a* of the Tablīghī Jamā'at movement to operate in the area.

The relationship between Haji Zaynu and Haji Musa began in the 1960s when they were part of Grand Anwar Masjid, one of the oldest *masjids* (mosques) in Addis Ababa. Haji Musa and Haji Zaynu were good friends and played significant roles in the history of Tablīghī Jamā'at in Ethiopia. Firstly, Haji Musa was willing to be the first *amir* for the Tablīghī Jamā'at movement while it was operating at Grand Anwar Masjid. Secondly, Haji Musa was willing to move the Tablīghī Jamā'at work to Zaynu's masjid in the 1970s, where Zaynu was the founding *imām*.

Zaynu provided all the necessary support for the work of the Tablīghī Jamā'at movement. He would travel to places where the *da'wa jamā'a* (team members of the Tablīghī work) were arrested because of the work of *da'wa,* and stand at government offices and police stations to defend those who were arrested, declaring, "These are my children. I will be the guarantor for them." In most cases, they were released. His diplomatic skills proved very helpful in dealing with officials at all levels. On occasion, he would express fury at any infringement of religious rights on the part of the officials.

Zaynu was widely held in high respect. Whenever any *masjid* leaders were hesitant to welcome the work of the Tablīghī Jamā'at movement and the Tablīghīs claimed "we are children of Haji Zaynu or Haji Musa," the masjid leaders would welcome them and open their mosques to them in order to facilitate the work of the movement. Zaynu's and Musa's names became like passports, allowing the *dais* (Tablīghī missionaries) to move easily from place to place.

In 2011, Haji Zaynu initiated the move to build a new five-storey complex that contained a mosque and the *markaz* (headquarters).

The years 2020 and 2021 will be remembered as very challenging years in the history of the world as the COVID-19 pandemic shut down entire countries, resulting in social isolation and unprecedented travel restrictions, affecting all religious gatherings and causing over 3 million deaths.

The Tablīghī Jamā'at response to COVID-19 varied. The Tablīghīs gathering in New Delhi, India created a serious controversy known as 'The Nizamudin-Controversy', which began on 13 March 2020. The Ministry of Health circular stated that 'Coronavirus is NOT a Health Emergency' and lockdown was not announced until 25 March. Meanwhile, there were a number of large gatherings of Tablīghī Jamaat leaders who came from different corners of the world for an assembly which took place from 13 to 15 March 2020 in New Delhi. The government of India accused the Tablīgh leaders of violating the government law by going ahead with the meeting. Of those who were present at the Tablīgh meeting, a few people died and many tested positive for COVID-19. The Tablīghī Jamaat gatherings were viewed as one of 'India's major virus hot spots' after thousands flocked to an Islamic religious centre in Nizamuddin's west neighbourhood.

By contrast, the government of Ethiopia consulted with Muslim religious leaders and the Ethiopian Inter-Religious Council, following which all religious gatherings were banned. The Tablīghī Jamaat Markaz came up with a decision to limit those sitting together or *khuruj* (going out) for the work of Tablīgh to three people.

The Gurāgēs

Introduction

The Gurāgēs are at the heart of the Tablīghī Jamā'at movement in Ethiopia. As business people and traders, the Gurāgēs are scattered all over the country, although their homeland extends to the Awash River in the north, the Gibe River (one of the tributaries of Omo River) to the west and Lake Ziway to the east, in the semi-mountainous region in Southwest Ethiopia, about 150 miles southwest of Addis Ababa.

The Gurāgē people are thought to have originated in the northern parts of what is currently Eritrea although some argue that they came from Saudi Arabia. Linguistically, the Gurāgē people relate to the Semitic language family and are regarded as an ethnic group.

The migration of the Gurāgē people to the northern parts of Ethiopia (then Eritrea) was led by Azmach Sebihat of the king's army, and they settled in north Gurāgē while a remnant army of Ahmad Gragn (the left-handed) remained in Wolane. The Silti and Azarnat Barbare Gurāgēs came from Barbara and Harar in the eastern parts of Ethiopia. Those who reside at Lake Ziway came from southern parts of Arabia.

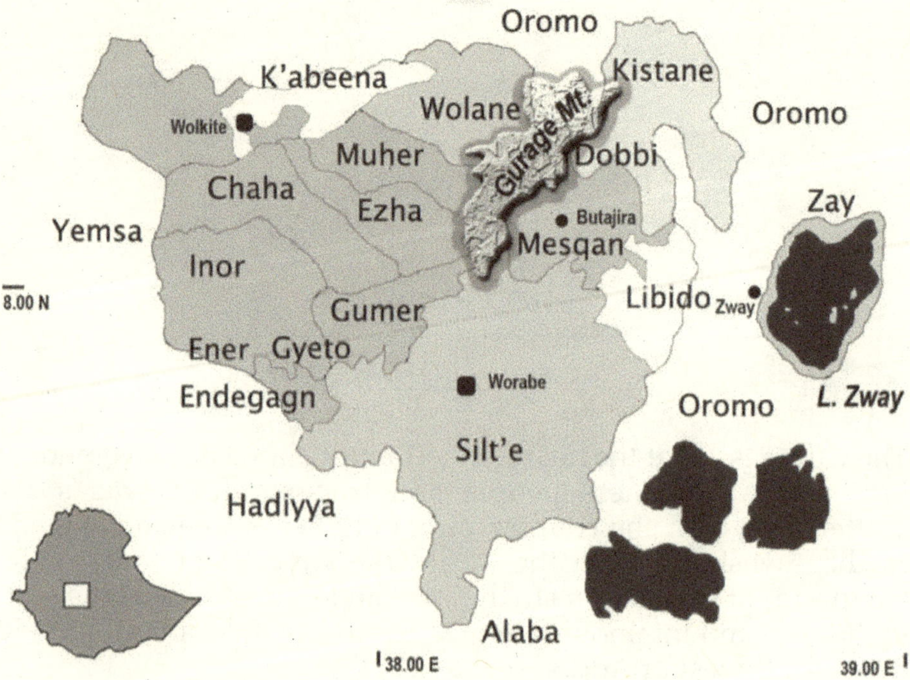

Map of Gurāgē and Silti Zones

The Gurāgē ethnic group can be divided into three in terms of religious affiliation. The Silti are a Muslim people; they are successful traders and contributed significantly to Ethiopia's economy and commercial activities. The Soddo Kistane have been followers of the Ethiopian Orthodox (Täwahïdo) Christianity for centuries. The Sebat Bet (Gurāgē) used to follow an indigenous religion represented by 'Waq' and converted to Islam and Christianity during the 20th century.

Tribal identity is part and parcel of the Gurāgē community, whether they are Muslims or Christians. The Gurāgēs are not only loyal to their bigger ethnic identity, they are also loyal to their tribal and smaller clan identity, to the extent that marriage within the same clan is prohibited. Gurāgēs are very meticulous about food preparation, particularly raw meat and its preparation with various seasonings. It is said that 'wherever the Gurāgēs are, there is meat!' Cheese, spinach, butter, homemade bread and cereals are always available and they are able to provide for themselves as well as guests.

The belief systems of the Gurāgēs are highly interwoven with indigenous traditions, including *Waq* (the sky god), *Boža* (god of lightning) and *demuwamit* (god of fertility). Such traditions take precedence over religious identity. Though Islam and Christianity are spreading among the Gurāgē people, it is very difficult to avoid indigenous traditions and practices that have been in place for years. Significant numbers of the Gurāgēs prefer to preserve the older beliefs and practices.

The Gurāgēs are not only agriculturalists but also intelligent and industrious workers, many of whom have settled in Addis Ababa where the word Gurāgē had different connotations, including 'porter.' Several years ago, anyone in Addis Ababa wishing to hire a porter, shouted "Gurāgē! Gurāgē!" since porters were mostly Gurāgēs. The Gurāgēs felt offended at this and protested to the government against such usage. As a result, the appellation "Gurāgē!" was forbidden, and instead the name "Kuli!" is now used for porters. Currently, the connotation of the word Gurāgē includes someone who works hard and is always looking to make a profit.

Internal migration (*fanonäti*) is common among the Gurāgē community. Since 1900, Gurāgēs started migrating to the urban areas, particularly Addis Ababa. In 1910, the number of *fano* (migrant) Gurāgēs was 2,000, constituting 3% of the total Addis Ababa population. In 1984, this increased to 255,000 or 18%. However, in the 21st century, the number living and working in Addis Ababa is estimated to be about one million, representing 16% of the total population of Addis Ababa. In the 1950s, there was no migrant (*fano*) Gurāgē with a licensed residence and business of his own in Addis Ababa except Sheikh Yusuf, who owned a property very near to the city council in the city centre. Currently, many Gurāgēs own houses, multiple businesses, commercial stores and luxury vehicles. Some of the reasons for migration (*fanonätï*) include scarcity of farmland, lack of modern farming, extended family ties in urban and rural areas and looking for betterment of their lifestyle.

The process of out-migration in the Gurāgē area is described locally as *fanonätï*, while the out-migrants are referred to as *fano*. The Gurāgēs are one of the most urban-orientated people groups in Ethiopia. *Fanonätï* refers to migration for economic reasons from the rural Gurāgē land to Addis Ababa and other urban areas. Gurāgēs are always on the move. Migration from the rural to the urban is part and parcel of their lifestyle. *Fanonätï* and *fano*, in the Amharic language, have a different meaning, however, which carries a political connotation, mainly as a migrant youth combatant. In August 2021, war was going on in the northern parts of Ethiopia and those who joined the war, non-formal army youth groups from the Amhara region, are known as '*fano*.' In times of peace, *fano* means the one who works on his farm, and during times of war, he becomes a soldier. But, within the Gurāgē community and language, the term *fano* refers to an economic migrant and has nothing to do with war or a political agenda.

The reality of the scarcity of farmland and migration stories of the Gurāgēs are highly significant. Beyond helping us understand the circumstances of migration, they also provide valuable insights into the larger contexts in which new Islamic renewal movement patterns evolved. Though the Gurāgēs migrate mainly for economic reasons, they immediately become involved in small business activities, including shoe-shining, retail and shopkeeping; they are not involved in social disturbances. The Gurāgēs also commit themselves to practising their religious duties, whether as Muslims or Christians.

In the 1950s and 1960s, the Gurāgēs operating small businesses faced intense competition with expatriate traders. These traders were mainly the Yemenite Arabs who monopolised major commercial activities and some of the small kiosks in Addis Ababa. They were called '*ārab-bet,*' to indicate the shopkeepers ('*ārab*' refers to the Arabs and '*bet*' to the house). The government was in favour of the Yemenis because they were strong financially and were taxpayers. In the Yemenis' struggle to compete with the Gurāgē traders, they arranged for the arrest by the police of any Gurāgē found selling items around the Yemenite shops, who were then jailed for a two-week period. Upon release, they had to pay a fine. However, despite all of the setbacks, the *fano* (migrant) Gurāgēs thrived in expanding their businesses and finally replaced the Yemenite Arabs in the commercial sector of Addis Ababa by the 1950s.

Migration is encouraged in Islam because it gives more opportunities to spread Islam to the area where migrants are going to settle. The Gurāgēs always represent the top numbers of those who migrate among Ethiopians. When the Gurāgē Muslims leave their homeland they consider themselves travellers of Allāh (*ya llāh musāfir*) and believe that Allāh will help them in all aspects of life.

The Addis Ababa Mosques

The first three mosques in Addis Ababa are historically connected to the work of the Tablīghī Jamā'at movement. The first mosque of Addis Ababa was built in 1906 at Aware, near Emperor Menelik II's palace. It was founded by Haji Wale Muḥammad, an Indian Muslim architect, who came with his family from India and worked on the construction of Emperor Menelik II's palace and Gibi-Gabriel (St Gabriel) Orthodox Täwahïdo Church for the Emperor. It was built on a piece of land given by Emperor Menelik and named Haji Wale Muḥammad Masjid after him.

The second mosque, Al-Nur Masjid, was founded in 1916 by the Qatbaré sheikh Issa Hamza (1875–1948), who migrated from the Gurāgē area to Addis Ababa, and by Yemeni Arab traders. Amira Kedir, who wrote her thesis on the Qatbaré sheikh, states:

> Brilliantly realizing the absence of a reasonable mosque in the capital and the eventual consequence this would bring against the Muslim believers, the Qatbaré Sheikh [Issa Hamza] once created cordial relations with the Yemeni Arabs so as to resolve the problem step by step. Accordingly, the Qatbaré Sheikh, after securing the *Jam'a* prayers in the residence of the Yemeni *Tujjars* [traders] asked if they would extend their solid support for constructing a mosque. The Yemeni Arabs had assured him that there were no difficulties if the authorization of such construction and a sizable plot of land was secured from the government side. The Qatbaré Sheikh did not waste his time.

Al-Nur Mosque was established in 1916 during Empress Zäwditu's time at Banin-Säfär, Piassa, where the City Council is located, very near to the municipality by the effort of the well-known Qatbaré Sheikh, Issa Hamza. Issa Hamza had a good relationship with Fitawrari Habtegiorgis, Minister of Defence, one of the influential leaders within the Ethiopian administration who was supportive of building the mosque, although he prohibited the construction of the minaret which would be very visible from every corner of the city. Habtegiorgis was known for his policy of religious tolerance and justice. Bahru Zewde, in his recent book on Habtegiorgis's biography, states:

> [Sixteen] Orthodox believers left their beliefs and joined the Protestant believers facing trial before the court. Many of the judges were expressing statements in favour of cutting their hands and legs, or hanging, or beating them publicly. This was expressed in the presence of Lij Iyasu (the then prince of Ethiopia as successor of Emperor Menelik) and Habtegiorgis. But Habtegiorgis said 'There is no law which says, someone who chose a different religion must be punished physically' and saved the 16 Protestants

In the 1930s, the great Al-Anwar Mosque was established as the third mosque in Addis Ababa with the help of the Italians (Mussolini personally saw to its completion) in the Marcato area which was, and still continues to be, the centre of trade and commerce for the capital and the country. The Italians had been instrumental in subsidising its construction and were supportive in rebuilding many Islamic institutions – not only this one but also hundreds of other mosques throughout Ethiopia at the time of the Italian occupation (1936–1941).

Gurāgēs and the Kikiyans' Influence in Trade at Marcato, Addis Ababa

From 1940 to 1980, the Kikiyans had a prominent name and commercial history, including building between 300 and 400 stone-built shops in the middle of the Marcato, a marketplace in Addis Ababa. This was celebrated in a rhyme: '350 are the shops of the Kikiyans, drag yourself around Piassa (to see and enjoy them); 400 are the shops of the Kikiyans, drag yourself around Marcato (to see and enjoy them).'

One man, Saleh Kikiya, enjoyed practising acts of generosity. He established a school in Massawa, his birthplace, and opened a mill in order to cover the cost of the school. His Muslim background did not prevent his desire to support Orthodox Christian projects as well. It is widely believed that his contribution to building Addis Ababa's great Anwar Mosque in the 1930s was substantial. He also covered one-third of the building costs of a school named after Häyïläsïlase I, now called the Kotebe Metropolitan University. This generous act by a private donor – probably the first of its kind – paved the way for the proliferation of aid organisations such as the Häyïläsïlase I Foundation for Humanitarian Organisation and many others.

This Kikiyan company had a great name in Marcato for 40 years but this declined after the death of the 53-year-old Saleh Ahmad Kikiyan in 1958. The younger Kikiyan brother, Usman Ahmad Kikiyan, died in 1979 and after that the Kikiyan heirs lost all their property, including their house in the middle of Marcato (Mars Hotel), due to the Marxist Policy of the Military Junta (Derg). Saleh had five children and was buried at his birthplace, Hirgigo Massawa. Usman, father of ten children, was buried in Kolfe Muslim Cemetery in Addis Ababa. The Kikiyans have been good friends and had excellent relationships with the Gurāgēs which, in large part, is due to the Gurāgēs' involvement in trade and commerce.

Since 1900, repetitive cycles of famine and drought have made Ethiopia one of the poorest countries in the world. This has caused internal migration, forcing people to beg on the streets of Addis Ababa and beyond. The author was born and raised in Addis Ababa, in the city centre, in a place called Piassa, which is a meeting place for people with different ethnic backgrounds, including Gurāgēs. He was never aware of seeing a single Gurāgē wandering around begging, which the Gurāgē culture discourages. The work and business ethics of the Gurāgēs are exemplary among many Ethiopians and one of the Gurāgē sayings depicts this trend: 'Unless coming and goings happened to Wolkite (capital town for Gurāgē Zone) and Waliso (another town near to Wolkite), how can someone find money? Just by checking his pocket.'

The Gurāgēs hold leadership positions at all levels in the Tablīghī as *Jamā* members, *amirs,* leaders (*mïdïbï, halaqa*) and members of the council (*shūrā)* for the Häbäša Markaz.

Butajira was chosen to host the first historic gathering of Tablīghī Jamā'at of 'Häbäša[3] Ijtima because it is a peaceful area with a good reputation for the coexistence of different religions with a good infrastructure. It was also seen as a fulfilment of the prophecy from the early fathers, including Qatbamre Sheikh Isa Hamza and Haji Musa Kikiyan who both stated that Butajira town will host *alims* (Musli scholars) and *Mashāikhs* from all over the world. The Gurāgēs, particularly the Silte-Gurāgēs, were

[3] Häbäša is a term referring to Ethiopians in Islamic literature.
'Häbäša,' which means 'people of mixed blood.' (Sudan Tribune, 18 February, by Magn Nyang 2009).

instrumental in the meeting; 65,000 people were registered participants for the event and the number of participants outside the stadium equalled those inside the stadium.

Many people from 180 countries were invited. The programme featured *Subhi bayan* (morning teaching) followed by *ahwal* (reports) from different parts of the country. At the end of the meeting, 240 people committed themselves to do *khuruj* (going out) to other countries travelling abroad for *da'wa*.

Teaching, Structure and Operation of Tablīghī Jamā'at in Ethiopia: Tablīghīs on the Move

Tablīghī Jamā'at is part of Sunni Islam, and is affiliated to the Hanafi Islamic School of jurisprudence. Sunni[4] is the largest of the main branches of Islam claiming an estimated 85% of Muslims all over the world. The Hanafi School is more Asian and allows for personal reflection and practices that can be considered as guidance and which sometimes leads to religious practice or *ṭarīqa* (path). In this case, it was a practice very much observed in the life of Ilyas, the founder of Tablīgh and his followers.

Tablīghī Jamā'at calls Muslims to the renewal of Islam and operates in towns and rural areas, where it faces opposition from the Salafis and Wahhabis, who are well established among the Oromo people. Salafis and Wahhabis consider Tablīghīs as a cult or a sect but Tablīghīs themselves consider their beliefs and practices to be part of Islam, with the exception that they view themselves as a group that works hard to bring Islamic renewal based on the Qur'ān, Ḥadīth and old traditions of the *ṣaḥāba*

[4] The Sunnis are the largest branch of the Muslim community, at least 85 percent of the world's 1.2 billion Muslims. The name is derived from the Sunnah, the exemplary behaviour of the Prophet Muḥammad. All Muslims are guided by the Sunnah, but Sunnis stress it, as well as consensus.

(Companions of Muḥammad). This is done mainly through the *sifatu sitta* (six principles) of Tablīghī Jamā'at teaching, which was developed in the 1920s by Mawlana Muḥammad Ilyās Khandhalwi and his successors.

The Tablīghī Jamā'at movement has its own structures and communications to help its followers and to invite others in the day-to-day operation and is strategically organised from grassroot level to global connections in terms such as *yabet ta'līm* (homestead study), *masjid* (mosque), *müdibï* (group), country, regional and global *markazes* (headquarters).

The Tablīghī Jamā'at movement and its followers always proclaim that they are promoting an apolitical movement. However, individuals are active in politics and sometimes suggest critical ideas on situations in Ethiopia without representing the Tablīghīs as a group. The Tablīghīs prefer non-confrontational relations with the Islamic jurisprudences, including Hanafi, Malik, Shafi and Hanbali. They consider these schools of law as the four breasts of a cow and are not interested in discussing deep Islamic theology.

The Arabic language, blended with Amharic, is widely used in the Tablīgh movement. Other local languages are used as necessary, including Gurāgē, Oromo and Somali. Translation is given at the *quarterly mashūra* (religious leaders gathering) at the Häbäša Markaz (national headquarters for Ethiopia).

The majority of the *jamā* (team) members come from a Gurāgē ethnic background and are also sent out to neighbouring countries and more distant places such as India, Bangladesh and Pakistan. Such travel resulted in participants being exposed to additional teachings and practices which encourage the momentum of the Tablīghī Jamā'at movement as a national and international movement to convince the world that Islam has the answer to the questions of life.

The term 'Stealthy Legions' was first used to describe the Tablīghī Jamā'at by Alex Alexiev in 2005 in his journal article in *Middle East Quarterly*. He argued this from his study of recruitment of Tablīghī members for military training in Pakistan in the 1980s and Tablīghīs' involvement in a terrorist bombing in Casablanca in 2003. His explanation for the condemnation was based on Pakistani and Indian observers who believed that Tablīghīs were instrumental in founding Harakat ul-Mujahideen, a militant Islamic organisation in Pakistan in the 1980s and that in the 1980s, over 6,000 Tablīghīs received their training in Harakat ul-Mujahideen Camp for the Afghan War and joined Al-Qaeda.

Michael Nazir-Ali, a former Bishop in Pakistan before becoming Bishop for Rochester in Kent, addressed the 'World Summit: Persecuted Christians' in 2017, in Washington DC where he refers to Tablīghī Jamā'at in Pakistan. He stated:

"They say [the Tablīghī Jamā'at] they are not violent. I believe them. But the question is, does their form of extremism which may not be violent in itself, lead people to involvement in violence? It does, for not everyone, but a small number, that's enough."

Tablīghīs never considered themselves as an exclusive sect, although others have done so. They are forming their own believing community which shares significant values of Tablīghī teaching and lifestyle from its South Asian roots.

Tablīghīs in Ethiopia have created a community of believers and the metaphor of 'The Family' is frequently employed, with members calling each other brother or sister and the leaders, Mother or Father. This way of adding 'brother' as a title before the names of believers in the Ethiopian context is also common among Protestant Christians.

The Tablīghīs' teachings and lifestyle are based on the six principles (*sifatu sita*) of the Tablīghī Jamā'at and the teachings on the 20 etiquettes (*adabs*), which they claim developed from the Ḥadīth and lives of the Companions (*hayatu saḥābas*).

In August 2014, the author had a chance to travel with the Tablīghī Jamā'at in Ethiopia for 42 days to understand its teaching, structure and operation as a participant observer. He was given permission to join the *jamā'a* (team) of Muslims who are committed to following in the footsteps of the Prophet to bring Islamic renewal through their mission. The majority of the *jamā'a* members were ethnic Gurāgēs, including the *amīr* (leader).

During this trip, he developed a good relationship among the Tablīghīs. And when asked by the leaders to accept Islam before joining, his response was:

"I am here to do my research, not to accept Islam. If I accept Islam, then, how can I be fair in my research journey?"

This was accepted, although his Tablīghī friends promised to continue praying for him to accept Islam.

Tablīghīs try to avoid documentation and the movement, like Ethiopians' religious traditions in general, is deeply rooted in oral traditions. There is a Tablīghī saying: "Once something has been written it becomes dead." So their invitation to the author was, "If you want to understand what is going on in the world of Tablīghīs, just come and join us and see." While he was travelling with the *jamā'a* he took notes, paying close attention to what they do, how they do it and why they do it. Apart from the teaching in the mosques, he participated in several roles as one of the *jamā'a* members. This included *ziyara* (visiting Muslim homes), *khidma* (purchasing food items and cooking), *ḥirāsa* (guarding) and taking part in *ta'līm* (study group), reading work from the English version of *faza'il al amal* (the Tablīghī text) and translating it into Amharic. In addition to this, he was involved in studying the Qur'ān, the *ḥadīth* and *hayātu saḥābas* (the story of the Companions of Muḥammad) with the help of the *amīr,* who is a very experienced Tablīghī.

According to the etiquettes of eating (*adab al-ta'ām*), proper use of resources is encouraged and is believed to bring about blessings. At the end of every meal, eating the leftovers from the dish as well as the food on the mat and licking fingers were routinely practised. According to the *ḥadīth,* wasting food (*isrāf*) is considered unlawful.

Tablīghī Teachings in Ethiopia

The Tablīghī teachings in Ethiopia, based on oral transmission, emphasise the six principles (*siffatu sitta*) of the Tablīghī Jamā'at. These are considered as the six marvellous virtues of the Companions (*ṣaḥāba*) of Prophet Muḥammad and there are now little booklets in the Amharic language to explain these. When Tablīghīs teach the six points, they stick with the most important points, although the emphasis differs with different teachers. Although most Orthodox Islam teaching is included, two of the Five Pillars of Islam are neglected, the teachings of *Hajj* (pilgrimage to Mecca) and *zakāt* (almsgiving). From the Six Articles of Faith, believing in the Books and Angels are not dealt with, leaving the Tablīghīs vulnerable to critics who sometimes state that they wish to replace the Six Articles with their six points.

The Tablīghīs' Six Virtues or Principles (Sifatu Sita)

The first principle of the Tablīghīs, Kalīma Tayyiba/*qal-tawhid* (elsewhere known as *la ilaha ilelahu Muḥammadun Rasul lilah),* focuses on the oneness of God (*qal-tawhid*). There is no one except Allāh, whom we subdue when we face and are passing through suffering, or whenever we are in need of His help. Our leader is Muḥammad, the messenger sent for the world, and no one could come after him. Allāh has the power and ability to help us without any help or causes from the creatures. As part of the first virtue, ratifying Muḥammad as a messenger is absolutely vital. To reach to prosperity and success (*falāh* and *najāḥ*), one must believe in the tradition (*sunna*) of Prophet Muḥammad and follow his footsteps to make his sunna alive. Not observing the life-style of the Prophet Muḥammad will lead one to be unsuccessful, bankrupt and experience destruction. The benefit of saying this creed is paradise (*Jannah*). "If a person's last words are *la ilaha ilelahu,* the person will enter paradise," said the Prophet Muḥammad. The reason for saying *Muḥammadun Rasul-ilah* is to change our ways and imitate the example of the Prophet.

The second virtue is prayer (*ṣalāt*), from which we take benefit from the safe box of Allāh (*khāzin*). "If you have a river which flows before your gate and wash five times a day, would you have any dirt on you?" the Prophet asked his Companions. Five times daily prayer (*ṣalāt*) will gain pardon for the small sins. *Ṣalāt* is the key for paradise (*Jannah*), and the key for *ṣalāt* is purification and ceremonial washing (*wudu*). Prayer demands patience and it is necessary to perform the prayer in an organised way, with humility and fear (*khush'* and *khud'*) as well as demonstrating a practical interpretation of submitting to Allāh. Prostrating should be done in an organised and fearful way.

The third virtue of the Tablīghīs is knowledge and remembrance (*'ilm* and *dhikr*). The purpose of knowledge (*'ilm*) is to submit to Allāh in a comprehensible way and to identify what is permitted and what is prohibited (*halal* and *haram*). The benefit of the former is walking in the light rather than the darkness. The purpose of the latter is to discard anything we depend on and to invite the greatness of Allāh within us. Knowledge (*'ilm*) is explained in a way that enables us to lead our life according to *sharī'a*. Also, the knowledge of *sharī'a* helps us to understand the will of Allāh, and how to perform Allāh's command, and tells of the blessing through fulfilling this command in all matters of life.

The fourth virtue of the Tablīghīs is teaching respect to all Muslims (*Ikramel Muslim*) and observing the justice or truth (*haq*) of the creatures. This includes loving our brothers because of Allāh. The purpose is to preserve our *haq* before Allāh, Glorified He is exalted (*Subhanahu wa-ta'ala*). There are two infamous incidents of two women from the Ḥadīth that were repeatedly mentioned throughout the 40-day *da'wa* tour. There was a lady who had been practising adultery (*zina*) for 40 years. But once, when she was thirsty, she went to a spring to drink water. There she saw a dog who was thirsty and was trying to satisfy himself by licking the soft, wet dirt. She brought water using her shoes and gave it to the dog. Because of this act, Allāh permitted her to enter paradise (*Jannah*). Another lady, who had been obeying Allāh for 40 years, tied up her cat at home, left for shopping and forgot her cat. She did not provide food or untie her cat so that the cat could find its provision (*rizq*) and in the process the cat died. Allāh condemned that lady to hell (*jahannam*). These didactic stories tell us the earnest longing of Ethiopian Tablīghīs for higher moral values here on earth and the 'not yet.' The purpose of honouring Muslims is to create strong bonds of love between Muslims. It is important never to offend a Muslim with hands or tongue. It is important to beautify ethics and give more attention to preserve the Muslim truths (*al-ḥaqq*).

The fifth virtue of the Tablīghīs' teaching is loyalty and intention (*Ikhlās Niya*), whereby our work needs to be acceptable to Allāh. In order to do that, whatever we do should be done in a qualified way. "Even if your job is little, ya Mua'az, you have to do your work in excellence," said the Prophet. This part of the six principles (*siffatu sitta*) is always brief. This was also considered as the fifth characteristic of the Companions of the Prophet (*ṣaḥāba*). The purpose of this characteristic is to accomplish work in sincerity (*ikhlāṣ*) for the sake of Allāh.

The sixth and last principle is a call to Islam in the way of Allāh (*daʿwa ilalah khuruj fi-sabililah*), recognising that we are a worshipping community (*daʿwa* and *ibāda*) for Allāh. "*Ya* Ali, if you are given the red camels, it is better to be a cause for guidance (*ḥidāyat*) to one of your brothers," said the Prophet. The main purpose for going out in the way of Allāh (*khuruj fi sabililah*) is to correct ourselves, not others. This is also considered the sixth characteristic of the Companions of the Prophet (*ṣaḥāba*). According to the Tablīghīs' booklet of the Amharic language version, the purpose of a call to Islam and going-out (*da'wa and Tablīgh and khurūj*) is to make alive the Islamic faith (*Dīn al-Islām*) as a lamp spreading light. Through this effort, Islam will thrive and be extended.

In most cases, the Tablīghīs in Ethiopia teach and convey all these messages orally but occasionally they use their little booklet in order to follow the sequences.

The overall teaching of Orthodox Islam is summarised with the five pillars of Islam: *shahāda* (affirmation), *ṣalāt* (five times daily prayer), *sawm* (fast), *zakāt* (almsgiving) and the *Hajj* (pilgrimage). It can also be summarised with the six beliefs of Islam: tawhid (the oneness of Allāh), Angels, Prophets, Books, the predestination of Allāh and belief in the Last Day. The Tablīghī Jamā'at's first and second points are similar with *tawhid, shahāda* and *ṣalāt*. However, the other four points are not found in the teachings of Orthodox Islam. The main points of Tablīghī Jamā'at teachings are very clear, simple and have no contradiction with Orthodox Islam, even though they are considered as *bida* (innovation) by *Salafis*. One informant from Salafi deems the whole Tablīghī Jamā'at teachings and operations heretical and regards the six points of Tablīghī Jamā'at as a replacement for the five pillars of Islam.

Ta'līm (study group) and Home-Based Ta'līm (the Breath of the Movement)

Ta'līm is a study group organised to seek knowledge with the aim of recognising the benefits of good ethics and the harmfulness and distraction of bad ones. The purpose of *ta'līm* is to prepare hearts to be touched by the speech of Allāh and Prophet Muḥammad and also to understand the full knowledge of the Islamic faith (*Dīn*) in order to create a genuine feeling of appreciation. The Tablīghīs sit in a small group and read from the Qur'ān, *ḥadīth,* Faza'il-e-al amal and *hayatu Saḥāba* (stories of the Companions of the Prophet) to learn from the lifestyle of the early days of *Saḥāba* (Companions of Muḥammad). *Ta'līm* could take place at a mosque or *markaz* (Tablīghī Jamā'at centre/ headquarters) as well as at homes of respective families.

Ta'līm has three goals in the life of *dā'īs* (Tablīgh/the one who does *da'wa*): i) to improve the ways of reading the Qur'ān in a manner of correct accent (*tajwidal* Qur'ān); ii) to develop practising good deeds through the reading of virtue of good deeds (*Faza'il-e-al amal*) from the book written by Maulana Muḥammad Zakariyya, one of the Indian frontline Tablīgh leaders; and iii) to remember the story of *Saḥābas* in light of the six principles in a way helpful to those who actively participate in the work of *dāʿīs*. These talks and teaching materials are recited, chanted and discussed in many *ta'līm* sessions.

According to the Tablīghī Jamā'at's, where *ta'līm* is taking place, there will be blessing (*barakah*) and light (*nūr*). Abdulhadi, *amir* in the 40-days *da'wa* tour, explained the need for *ta'līm* by quoting from the early days of Islam and connecting to the present days. "In the early days of Islam, Omar, who once tried to kill Muḥammad, accepted Islam because of home-based *ta'līm*. The *masjid* of the Prophet was under the palm tree." Behind legitimisation of various *Tablīghī* practises there is a creative appropriation and reinterpretation of events and rituals of early Islam from the conversion of Omar through *ta'līm* to give a rationale for going around and going out (*jaula* and *khurūj*). There is a saying among the Tablīghīs in Ethiopia in relation to knowledge (*'līm*): "From thousands of discernment (*karāmā'*), integrity (*istiqāma*) is much better."

There are instructions for those reading to the group. The Qur'ān and Ḥadīth should be read repeatedly twice. Let the reader read the given commentaries (*sharḥs*). He should avoid adding his own opinions and emotions. Whenever the reader mentions the name of Allāh, let him say "Great is His Majesty (*jalla jalālhu*) and His sovereignty reigns." When the reader mentions words of mercy, he needs to motivate his listeners. This gathering (*ḥalaqa*) is a place where important counsel is spoken. It is not a place for debates on scientific applications but the application of the *sharī'a* (*fiqh*).

The Tablīghīs have detailed rules and regulations for the practical operation of their mission, summarised with an oral presentation called the 20 *adabs* (the 20 etiquettes) which are divided into five main categories. The nature of these etiquettes is in line with the Sunnah of the Prophet Muḥammad in the Qur'ān. The main five divisions of the *adabs* include: i) things to be maximised; ii) things to be minimised; iii) things not to be neglected; iv) things not to be interfered with; and v) things not permitted.

(i) Things to be maximised:

- *da'wa* (a call to Islam) must be maximised. The work of *da'wa* is good and no one can reach it, just as one cannot reach the goodness of Allāh. Ethiopian Muslims in general and Tablīghīs in particular know the importance of participating in *da'wa. Ta'līm* must be maximised at all places, including mosques and homes, in groups and on an individual basis. Though the Tablīghīs are not high-level scholars, seeking knowledge is crucial in the day-to-day life and they are encouraged to maximise their effort to practise the necessary virtues of Tablīghīs.
- *dhikr* (remembrance) through reciting the name of Allāh must be maximised. The Tablīghīs always remember Allāh by reciting His name, striving to be far from the worldly and nearer to the hereafter.
- *khidma* (serving others) must be maximised. Serving others includes team members at *fi sabililah* (in the way of Allāh), the leader (*amir*) and all Muslims who are in need of *khidma*.

(ii) Things to be minimised:

- Do not eat too much.
- Do not sleep too much.
- Minimise coming and going into mosques.
- Minimise gossiping and worldly engagement.

(iii) Things not to be neglected:

- Obeying the leader (*amīr*) must not be ignored.
- Respect and give priority to the purpose of the team (*jamā'a*). Preserving the personal *tartib* (schedule) at all times.
- Respect the masjid disciplines.
- Patience (*sabr*) must not be ignored in any circumstances.

(iv) Things not to be interfered with:

- When the Tablīghīs are on *khurūj* (going out), talking about politics is officially forbidden, but one cannot be free from politics, and thinking about, reflecting on and discussing politics does take place.
- No interference in the issue of *khilafas* (disputes) on Islamic jurisprudence. It is important not to condemn others or be critical with Muslim friends who have a different understanding of the Ḥadīths.
- No interference in any issues of the mosques; no interference in *masjids haq* (belongings of mosques).
- No interference in the weaknesses of any particular area and arguments.

(v) Things not permitted:

- *isrāf* (profusion) is not allowed. Utilise resources wisely and economically. As one of the poorer countries in the world, civil war among brothers has been a great hindrance to the use of the limited resources of the country.
- Coveting (*ishrāf*) is not permitted.
- Taking your brother's belongings without permission is not allowed.
- Filthy and worldly talk is not allowed.

In Addis Ababa, there is an Islamic Training Centre called *ya-'Ubayy Firewoch ya-Qur'ān Hifz Maekel* (Fruit of Ubayy Qur'ān Memorisation Centre), named after Ubayy ibn Ka'b, the master of the reciters in the early days of Islam. This centre was established in 2004 and is a boarding school for 180 male students.

This centre has five branches in Addis Ababa. The main purpose of this centre is to help Muslims in their recitation of the Qur'ān but it also sends its students to *da'wa* tours as part of its field practical programme and as a requirement for graduation.

Tablīghīs' Operation in Ethiopia

Tablīghīs' operation in Ethiopia has some similarities with other countries but has developed its own way of doing things.

After Haji Musa, the first leader of the Tablīghīs, died in 2002, the leadership was organised in a more collective manner, with a committee exerting the overall responsibility. This practice of decision making is called *mashūra* (council), which is the heart of the movement.

The purpose of having a *mashūra* is to spread the Islamic faith and attributes (*din* and *siffat*) individually, at the family level, locally, nationally and globally. This includes preparing the children to be knowledgeable in memorising the Qur'ān (*ḥāfizal Qur'ān*), making the younger generation able to perform a call to Islam (*dais*), preparing women to be helpers of the Islamic faith (*Dīn*) and requiring properly veiled women (*mutahajibat*) and the elderly as those who do remembrance (*zakir*).

The *mashūra* serves as the heart of the Tablīghī Jamā'at movement and has a very interesting saying: "There is no meeting before a meeting and there is no meeting after a meeting." (No *mashura* before *mashūra* and no *mashūra* after *mashūra*.) A meeting before a meeting is a revolt and a meeting after a meeting is gossip. The leader (*amir*) elaborates on the purpose of the *mashūra* and invites each participant to ask questions or make comments. When the leader presents his idea, it is not a final decision but is open for discussion. However, at the end of the discussion, the leader's decision will be final. The purpose of *mashūra* is to discuss strategies for how Islam can be spread, both locally, nationally and internationally.

Interested applicants for the 40-days, four-months, or one-year *da'wa* tours would go to the national markaz, where their name would be registered. This would clarify the number of people participating and allow for appropriate planning.

Ethiopian Tablīghīs may commit themselves to go out of the country to India, Pakistan and Bangladesh for a minimum of four months and say, "I am ready for *merakiz*." There, they may attend the annual gatherings, where the number of attendees is second only to the Hajj of Mecca.

The Tablīghī structures are loose in nature and there are no paid staff. There is no limit to how long one can stay with the

Global Tablighī Jamā'at Structure

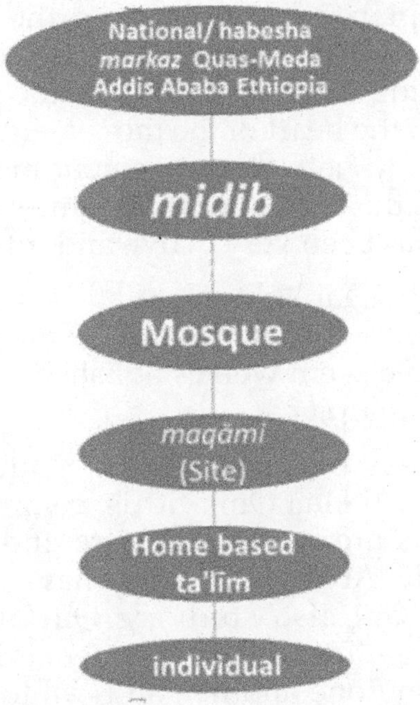

Ethiopia Tablīghī Jamā'at Structure

movement. Structurally, the approach is more bottom-up, not top-down but the upper level is ready to support as it is needed.

The Ethiopian *markaz* has six layers:

Each group (*mïdïbï*) has a different number of mosques in Addis Ababa and home-based *ta 'alim*, with over 500 *masjids* and *muṣallās* (mosques and prayer rooms) and over 13,000 home-based *ta'līm*. The number of mosques and prayer rooms and home-based *ta'lim* is set to continue to grow.

As the head of the Tablīghī Jamā'at movement, the role of the *mashūra* is invaluable for the Tablīghīs in Ethiopia and, as such, it is instrumental for smooth operation and accountability at all levels. The Ethiopian *mashūra* mirrors the global *mashūra* in Nizamudin, India as the integral part and epicentre of the movement. Nothing happens without the knowledge of the *mashūra*. However, the heart of the movement is *ta'līm*, which has different teachings to help the movement move forward. Given the oral culture of the region, oral transmission of the teaching-learning process has been very active and influential.

It is clear that the Tablīghī Jamā'at is well organised and structured at all levels. Though a massive missionary movement, Tablīghīs in Ethiopia seem well established with the potential to reach millions of Ethiopians.

The current President of the Ethiopian Islamic Affairs Supreme Council, Grand Mufti Haji Omar Idris, commented that, "These days, the Tablīghīs are becoming more and more involved in education. In Addis Ababa alone they have 60 Islamic schools" (*madrasas*). "They are also studying Qur'ān and have a few scholars among them. Today the movement is known by the work of visitation, helping one another, and call to Islam" (*ziyara* and *da'wa*).

Ethnography of Tablīghīs' Mobility 'The People of Visitation and Call to Islam (yaziyara-na yada'wa säwočī)': The Basis of the Tablīghī Jamā'at Movement

Introduction

The visitation *da'wa* tour and call to Islam are the vibrant part of the Tablīghī Jamā'at movement. In 2014, the author was granted permission to join the 40-days *da'wa* tour and the quarterly *mashūra* by the leaders at the Häbäša *Markaz*. He told them about his family background, that his father was half Yemeni and half Ethiopian and was a Muslim but converted to Orthodox Christianity after marrying his mother. Many of the relatives from his father's side are still in Yemen, Sanaa and Teez and are still Muslims. He also told them about his Master's degree research, which was on 'folk Islam in Wallo,' and his visit to places (*gatā*), where he had met the current Sheikh, Hajji Muhiddin Adam.

A friend of the author asked permission to take him on the 40-days *da'wa* tour (going out in the way of Allāh) *khuruj fi-sabililah,* starting at the beginning of Ramadan. This was agreed. The team was composed of 14 members (*jamā'a*), most of whom came from Addis Ababa, and each one of them was active in the Tablīgh work around their areas. Age-wise, most were in their teens, demonstrating how the Tablīghī movement is gaining ground with the younger generation in the urban areas. Even though the majority of the members were from the Gurāgē ethnic group, their command of Amharic was satisfactory.

Pre-*da'wa* tour preparation was required for joining the 40-days *da'wa* tour and everything was clearly explained to everyone at the Häbäša *Markaz*. Three speakers focused on discipline and abstaining from politics and religious arguments. They also focused on *salat* (prayer), reading the faza'il-e-al amal, Qur'ān and reading *al-fatiha, Khalima Toyba la-ilaha ilelahu Muḥammad rasul-ilah*. Special focus for the study session in groups (*ta'līm*) was in three parts: Faza'il-e- al amal, Qur'ān; Hayātu *saḥābas* (life of the Companions of the Prophet); and *sifatu sitta* (the six principles of Tablīghī). The team was told to be courageous in their individual activities, including doing remembrance (*dhikr*) 600 times per day – 300 times in the morning and 300 times in the evening; asking the forgiveness of Allāh (*Istighfār*) 200 times per day – 100 times in the morning and 100 times in the evening; and *Allāh-Musole Allāh-Muḥammade*, 200 times per day – 100 times in the morning and 100 times in the evening. Also, *Subhan-Allāh wala Hamdililah, walahu akbar la hawla wala qureta ila bila hi aliyu lazim*, 200 times per day – 100 times in the morning and 100 times in the evening. The five times of prayer, reading the Qur'ān, remembrance and casual prayer (*salat, qiryat, dhikr* and *dua'a*) must be taken seriously as part of the personal devotion.

Testimonies (*ahwal*) were heard from those who had returned from their *da'wa* tour. These were presented by their respective *amirs* as part of the guidance (*ḥidāya*) and as an encouragement for the novice Tablīghīs who were ready (*mustaid*) for the 40-days *da'wa* tour.

The speaker stressed the greatness of grace (*nii'ma*) in Islam which Allāh gave.

"Allāh sent 124,000 prophets (*anbiyas*), and all of the *anbiyas* brought a message that there will be an awakening from death. The purpose of the coming of the Prophet Muḥammad was to divide human beings into two groups: people for heaven (*Janet*) and people for hell (*Jahannam*). While you are on the going out (*khuruj*), don't touch any alcoholic drink, *khat* (a stimulant plant), and belongings which are not yours. If you chew *khat* and get excited you will lose control of your mind, which leads you to be disobedient to your leader (*amir*) and start doing *dhikr* (remembrance). Please don't touch *khat* at least for 40 days."

This part of the instruction implied that *khat* is not strictly forbidden in the world of Tablīghī in Ethiopia.

The teaching continued, relating that at Arafa, in Mecca, there could be over five million people gathered every year.

There were about six jobs for everyday activities and the group were to be sure to implement all of them: execute council (*mashūra*) according to etiquettes of council (*adab-mashūra*); listen to testimonies (*aḥwāl*); initiation for how to go forward; vision and planning (*fikr*); decisions (*fāiṣala*) which will be made by the *amir*; 24-hour programme (*tartib*); and study group (*jamā'a ta'lim*). The study group (*ta'lim*) has its own purpose, benefits and etiquettes. The purpose of *ta'lim* is to find light (*nūr*) and interest in heaven (*yaqīn*). The morning teaching (*subhi bayan*); the late afternoon teaching (*asar bayan*); etiquettes of sleeping (*adab-nawm*); etiquettes of eating (*adab-taam*); reading from the story of the Companions of the Prophet (*hayātu ṣaḥābas*); and treating others (*khidma*) were a part of the seemingly endless list of duties. On the one hand, it seemed like a military discipline in which everything must be done in accordance with the guidelines given by the hierarchy; on the other hand, it is still a religious practice that demands an iron discipline to implement all of the necessary expectations.

The quality of a good team leader (*amir*) is someone who would make his (*jamā'a*) team members busy with different activities and involve them with necessary responsibilities. The very reason for going out in the way of Allāh (*khuruj fi-sabililah*) is to correct bad characters and to embrace the good ones.

The speaker continued: "Please complete your *khuruj* with love (*muhaba*) and diligence. Between six and eight hours of sleep on *khuruj* is enough. If any problems are faced on *khuruj*, the place to call is the headquarters at Häbäša *Markaz*, nowhere else. Those who are ill and taking medicine should not go far. Work under the group (*mïdïbï*) you are in at your locality (*maqāmi*). Teach at the main gate of the mosques (*tamirel-masjid*). Go out for visitation (*ziyara*) and do home-to-home visits. Divide and organise the area where you work. Work hard for 40 days and win your soul (*nafsiya*).

"It is forbidden for a person on *fi-sabililah* to take a shower in the river, as being naked is totally unacceptable. Every day, stress was placed on treating others well (*khidma*) and not offending one's brother with bad words. The preparation of food was based on the contribution made, for 40 days, about 2,000 Ethiopian Birr ($100 USD). Distribute the money between three people. Keep it carefully and safely, and do not assign this responsibility to novice Tablīghīs."

This 40 days *da'wa* tour took place in the Oromia Region, Arsi Zone, which is considered a stronghold of Salafis, although the Sufi form of Islam also has a huge influence on the vast majority of the Arsi people who are situated to the southeast of Addis Ababa.

During the tour, 14 mosques and Tablīgh offices (*masjids* and *markazes*) were visited. In the mosques, individual praying and reading took place, which was expected to bring renewal for each of the *jamā'a* members. When leaving the *masjids,* the focus was on other people, calling them to the *masjids* so that they could be with the group and practise what the group were doing there. Public transportation was used for the journeys.

Post-Da'wa Tour Guidance (*ḥidāya*)

The post-*da'wa* tour guidance (*ḥidāya*) began with concluding remarks by the *amir,* Abdulhadi, for two hours.

He started by explaining issues in *mashūra* and the needs of the Muslim community. He then reiterated the Five Major Works (*Khamsa amal*) of consultation (*mashūra*); knowledge (*ta'lim*); spare time (*tafrig*); visiting and organisation (*maqāmi and intiqali*); and the monthly schedule (*tartib*). He continued without notes, talking from his heart and mind, and everyone felt like one family. The group moved to the Häbäša Markaz to present their testimonies (*ahwal*) and receive the final guidance (*ḥidāya*) before departing to their homes.

The daily routine of the 40-days *da'wa* tour was as follows: 5:00–5:40am devotion and prayer, both personal and congregational; 5:40–6:00am morning motivational talk (*fajr bayān*) in the mosque; 6:00–6:15am discussions on the greatness of Allāh in pairs (*infirād*); 6:15–6:30am council (*mashūra*); 6:30–7:00am a discussion on Islamic jurisprudence (*fiqh*) on practical matters such as ceremonial washing; and 7:00–9:30am sleeping time and preparation for the longer session to come. The afternoons were always set for going out for *da'wa (jaula*). Because it was the month of Ramadhan, they took food in the early mornings and evenings.

As one of the learning opportunities, at the everyday council (*mashūra*) meeting, the team (*jamā'a*) put the world map in its midst. Fixing our eyes on the world map on the wall or putting it in the midst of the *jamā'a* was a tradition for the Tablīghīs in Ethiopia. The *jamā'a* members, looking to the world map, in turn may say, "I want to see the supremacy of Islam in my life, in my family, in my mosque, in my country and all over the world." While officially not interested in politics, the longing for 'supremacy' indicates the political interest of the Tablīghīs, and without political involvement, reaching to the supremacy of Islam worldwide is unthinkable.

The motto of the Tablīghī Jamaat movement is simple: "Oh Muslims! Become Muslims." To become a good Muslim and fulfil the motto of the Tablīghī movement, practising Islam in the form of Tablīgh is vital. Explaining the six principles of Tablīghīs (*siffatu sitta*) is part of their formal and informal training and is demonstrated at every opportunity. When a study group (*ta'līm*) takes place, each one is expected to recite the *siffatu sitta*.

There is a great sense of imitation of the early days of Islam, such as trying to follow the example of the Prophet Muḥammad and the *ṣaḥāba*. Walking is the preferred method of travelling, sometimes over 20 kilometres a day. The promotion of leading a simple lifestyle is advocated. Sheikh Engineer Ali Khadir, is seen as the current *amīr* for the national *Häbäša Markaz*. He stated: "We should go on foot, for there are places which we cannot reach by aeroplanes, vehicles, ships or horses. Only the feet can get us anywhere." That's why home visitation is employed to fulfil the *da'wa* mission.

Nusra Jamā'a is a team of helpers ready to give support and encouragement to the formal *Jamā'a* (team) who already left for a different area of the country for the Tablīghī Jamā'at work. The purpose of organising and sending *Nusra Jamā'a* is to help the team who have been in the field for a long time and are tired, often with financial constraints.

Masturat is the women's involvement in the work of Tablīghī Jamā'at. Tablīghīs in Ethiopia, unlike elsewhere, are not doing well in *masturat* (participating women in *da'wa*). The goal is to produce women in contemporary Tablīghī Jamā'at' with six ideal characteristics: *dā'iya* (proselytiser); *'ābida* (pious believer); *muta 'allima* (teacher); *murabbiya* (educator); *khādima* (server); and *zāhida* (manage a simple life).

Women's involvement in the work of the Tablīghī movement seems slow due to social circumstances and cultural issues; however, progress has been made over the last few years.

Jaula is going around to call upon the local Muslims and beyond to attend the teachings at the nearby mosque. Someone who teaches and motivates people on how to accomplish *jaula* should explain the following four points in the right manner: i) The necessity of faith (*Dīn*) and the great value before Allāh; ii) The need and the purpose of *da'wa* must be explained; iii) The benefits of making the Islamic faith (*Dīn*) alive, as this general *jaula* is part of the strive of the Islamic faith; and iv) The disciplines of open and hidden *jaula.*

The *jaula* strategies explain how to relate the importance of the Islamic faith: anybody who holds the Islamic faith will only be successful here on earth and the hereafter. A person whose life is in line with Allāh's command and the sunna of the Prophet and develops his life through the Islamic faith will be successful here in this world and the hereafter. A person who does not have faith, or is half-heartedly faithful, faces a great loss in this world and the hereafter and finds himself in incomparable disaster.

Before Allāh, the best thing is faith. The very reason that Allāh created the heaven and the earth is the Islamic faith. So long as the Islamic faith is alive, the existence of the heaven and the earth will be preserved. Lacking the Islamic faith will put the existence of the world in danger. Truly, the Islamic faith is the soul for our physical body. If there is a soul in our physical being, all parts of the body will function properly. If there is no soul in the physical body, the body will become a dead body. So long as the Islamic faith is alive on earth, even partly, the earth continues its duties to benefit mankind. Rain continues raining; rivers continue flowing; plants continue growing and bearing fruit; and the sun and moon shine down properly. If there is no Islamic faith in the lives of people the worlds do not have existence. Someone who gives greater attention to the Islamic faith (*Dīn*), turns his whole life to the direction of the *Dīn* and holds the *Dīn* very strictly will earn success here on earth and the hereafter. Whoever works, donates and strives for the *Dīn*, puts the *Dīn* over the worldly (*dunyā*) and generally submits the totality of his life, including his time, knowledge and energy for the *Dīn*, has ratified success here on earth and the hereafter. A person who is poor or wealthy, woman or man, white or black, slave or lord, who says the Islamic faith is false and is out of the faith of Allāh, driven by his emotion and has chosen the life of this physical world, will be a loser in both worlds.

The greater before Allāh are Allāh's slaves. Allāh ordered the prophets to perform a higher struggle for the Islamic faith (*Dīn*). The best thing to perform before Allāh is to work hard for the *Dīn*. This is not difficult to understand. If there is any other thing that is the most loved before Allāh, prophets could have been ordered to do it.

This Muslim community (*umma*) of faith has been working hard to spread the *Dīn* through organising teams (*jamā'at*) and assigning armies of faith. For these reasons there has always been help, blessings and mercy from Allāh. People are flooding to the faith of Allāh. When this Muslim community (*umma*) started neglecting this holy purpose of spreading the *Dīn* and stopped sending teams (*jamā'at*) to the rest of the world, they were deprived of help from Allāh. Then the Muslim community faced failure and dishonour and disgrace before their enemies as a result of those who left their faith.

Allāh sent the prophets when times of corruption and adultery (*fāsid* and *zina*) increased and people's faith (*'aqīda*) and behaviour decreased. Because they had been immersed within a great immorality, the rulers at that time were not willing to lead them but dishonoured and despised the people. Allāh planned to deliver the people from this failure so He sent the Prophet Muḥammad as the Messenger. The Prophet started the *da'wa* movement with great energy, doing *jaula* day and night. The Prophet explained the greatness and sovereignty of Allāh, putting forth this message with great strength and authority. The lives of the Arabs changed and they grasped strong faith. They believed in the greatness and sovereignty of Allāh and were freed from evil practices.

The greatness of Allāh should always be explained as an introduction to Muslims when *jaula* takes place. The need for *da'wa* and the purpose of *jaula* must be clarified. The significance of *jaula* is briefly explained as part of the struggle (*jihūd*) in the process of spreading the Islamic faith in order to keep it alive (*Dīn al Islam*). Success here on earth and the hereafter is only through *Dīn al Islam,* so each one is expected to build their life in the line of *sunnah* (tradition of the Prophet) and the ordinance of Allāh. Muslims are called to invest their time and energy wholeheartedly towards their *Dīn*, like in the early days of *ṣaḥāba*

(Companions of Muḥammad), so this can be demonstrated through the effort of *da'wa.* All are members of the community of *Dīn* (faith) and are supposed to pray to Allāh to make *Dīn al Islam* great and supreme.

Etiquettes of Visitation and Going Around (Adabs of Ziyara and Jaula)

There are two main parts of etiquettes for the execution of *jaula.*

i) External: be in the spirit of prayer all the time, respect all the necessary traditions, control our eyes from what we see, be obedient to the *amir*, whenever we walk for *jaula*, walk on the right side of the road, move in *dhikr* (remembrance), *shukr* (thanksgiving) and *ṣabr* (patience), and keep quiet and do not make any talk or speech except the *mutakalim* (spokesman of the team). The external etiquettes of *jaula* which are not connected with the heart include prayer (*du'ā'*); I really do not understand how prayer could be an external etiquette, but this is the way the Tablīghīs see it. One must observe the traditions of the Prophet (*sunna*), control what you see, begin on the right side when making any movements to go around, be obedient to the leader of the team (*amir* of the *jamā'a*), do not be forgetful to remember and mention Allāh's name and do not speak to anyone except the assigned spokesman (*mutakallim*) at the time of *jaula.*

The Tablīghīs' movement is full of etiquettes which need to be observed at all times.

ii) Internal: strongly believe and trust Allāh that this *jaula* will play a greater role in influencing people and bring a life change to those who listen to it. Accomplish this *jaula* with a sincere and faithful manner, focusing on Allāh, and move around with the clean intention of rectifying ourselves. One must put on humility and a merciful character towards the *Ummat* (Muslim community), as well as maintain a constructive view: repent, feel sad and ask forgiveness from Allāh for anything neglected when we are doing *jaula.*

Upon return from *jaula,* ask Allāh for mercy and forgiveness (*istighfār*) for not accomplishing this holy work properly.

When introducing the work of Tablīghī, when *jaula* is taking place, the use of Arabic is encouraged but it is also necessary to translate the speech into Amharic, as most Muslims in Ethiopia do not understand Arabic.

There is a special way of explaining the work of Tablīghī to attract those who listen in Arabic and Amharic: "Peace be upon you. The reason we came to visit (*lamazayr*) you is for the sake of Allāh. You are our brothers through Allāh. All of us are the members of Islamic faith (*Dīn al Islām*). No prophet will be sent after the Prophet. All have a strong responsibility to make it live, protect and propagate Islam (*Dīn*) and to make Islam alive all over the world, reflecting (*fikr*) and discussing how to design the strategy for this."

> *When entering an area to perform jaula, the following etiquettes should be in place. Remember that all arrived at this particular town by the will and help of Allāh to make the effort (jihūd) of the Prophet Muḥammad come alive. Any thought reflected (fikrā) in our mind will be reflected in the area where we work. For this reason, we must sharpen our intention (niya) and reflection (fikrā). The main task before us, upon which we think and reflect, must be on the people of this area, how they can make the effort*

> *(jihūd) of the Prophet come alive and prepare them for the work of da'wa (a call to Islam) to go out (khurūj) for three, ten and 40 days, four months and, sometimes, for a year.*
>
> *One should perform a call to Islam, prayer, remembrance and worship, and we should involve ourselves by serving others (da'wa and du'ā, dhikr and 'ibāda, khidma) and do good things. When we enter the mosque, step first with our right foot and say this: "In the name of Allāh let peace be upon the Prophet. Oh, Allāh open the door of your mercy." Someone who has done ritual washing for prayer (wuḍū'), should then perform two cycles (rak'at) of prostration (sujūd) at the mosque. After that, we sit for a consultative meeting (mashūra). Speaking loudly and interfering with issues in the mosque is strictly forbidden.*

Da'wa, jaula and *ziyara* are all interconnected and demonstrated through visiting the area where the Tablīghī Jamā'at work is taking place to meet with people, wherever they are. This part of the work could be considered as the 'feet' of the movement. The main purpose of this movement is to call Muslims to be Muslims and the main actors are those who left their homes willingly to join this movement, aimed at bringing an Islamic renewal among Muslims in their localities and in areas where they are envisioned to be – in most cases cross-culturally within Ethiopia and cross-border.

Locating the Ethiopian Tablīghī Jamā'at in the Current Debate on Faith and Politics, Spirituality, Solidarity and Secretiveness of the Ethiopian Tablīghīs

The Ethiopian Tablīghīs are willing to send their girls to modern schools to have a secular education and they encourage other Muslims to do so, unlike the Pakistani Tablīghīs. Malala's story from Pakistan contrasts sharply with better gender relations and access to education in Ethiopia, which is due to the more egalitarian ethic of the Gurāgē compared to the cultural context of Tablīghī Jamā'at in South Asia.

Malala Yousafzai, a Pashtun[5], was born in Khushal Street, Swat Valley, North-West Frontier Province, Pakistan. Malala is known as an educational campaigner. The Mufti on Khushal Street, Mullah Ghulamullah, was a member of Tablīghī Jamā'at, a Deobandi group that holds a huge rally every year at its headquarters in Raiwind, near Lahore, attended by millions of people. The Mufti turned up at Malala's door with seven people,

[5] Malala Yousafzai is a Pakistani female education activist and the 2014 Nobel Peace Prize laureate. Awarded when she was 17, she is the world's youngest Nobel Prize laureate and the second Pakistani and the first Pashtun to receive a Nobel Prize.
Pashtun is one of the people groups in Pakistan. For most Pashtuns, it is a gloomy day when a daughter is born.

some other senior Tablīghīs, a mosque keeper, a former jihadi and a shopkeeper, and they filled the small house. "As a leader of the team, I am representing the Ulema and Tablīghīan and Taliban," Mullah Ghulamullah said, referring to not just one but two organisations of Muslim scholars, to give himself gravitas. "I am representing good Muslims and we all think your girls' school is *haram* [unlawful in the *sharī'a*] and blasphemy. You should close it. Girls should not be going to school," he continued. "A girl is so sacred she should be in purdah, and so private." So far, sending girls to schools is not an issue for Ethiopian Muslims in general and Tablīghīs in particular, who encourage education for girls.

The debate and conflict between the Tablīghīs and Wahhabis/Salafis can be summarised in three main categories. One, celebrating *mawlid*, the birth of Prophet Muḥammad. Two, interpretation of religious teaching and practices, including the six virtues/principles (*sifatu sita*) of Tablīghīs, as well as going far to accomplish religious duties for days, weeks and months without having an appropriate knowledge of Islam and neglecting their own families. Three, political involvement (less interest from the Tablīghīs, if not the hate of politics, but, more of an appetite from the Wahhabis).

One of the arguments between the Tablīghīs and Wahhabis/Salafis is the issue of celebrating *Mawlid*. "This ritual [*Mawlid*] celebration of the birth of the Prophet Muḥammad and his holy deeds is performed by the recitation of spiritual poems. It is a popular practice in Sufi Islam, but is firmly rejected by Salafis." Not only is it practised by the Sufis, it's also supported and promoted by the Tablīghīs, who always celebrate *Mawlid* commemorations. The majority of Tablīghīs practise the Tablīghī movement without sacrificing their traditional Sufi practices.

The debate on the birthday of Prophet Muḥammad (*Mawlid*) has been ongoing for a while in Ethiopia and is currently becoming more serious. Since 1806, Muslims in Ethiopia practised the *Mawlid* celebration in an organised way; Ethiopian Sufis have a special connection with the Prophet Muḥammad and his birthday, although Muḥammad did not order that his birthday should be celebrated.

The late Haji Muḥammad Sani Habib achieved making *Mawlid* an Ethiopian national holiday at the time of the Military Junta (*Derg*) in 1985; it was the most important gain for Islam after the revolution.

Debate on Islamic Knowledge

The Sufis in Ethiopia are known to chew *khat*[6] now and then. The Tablīghīs do not forbid *khat* chewing as the Wahhabi/Salafi do. The main reason for this is the Tablīghīs think that everything should be done little by little (*bitdaruj*). It should not be drastically overdone. Of course, at the time of a *da'wa* tour, it is strictly forbidden. But someone with a habit of *khat* chewing could join the *da'wa* team and attempt to state that he is permitted to have this bad habit. For Christian Abyssinians (Ethiopians), the use of *Chat* (*khat*) is typically Muslim, and the consumption of *Chat* (*khat*) is probably considered to be a sign of adherence to Islam.

The Sufis also practise tomb visits wherever the tombs of well-known *Sheikhs* are buried. The Wahhabis/Salafis are very much against this practice, unlike the Tablīghīs, who tolerate it.

---

[6] Khat or qat is a flowering plant native to Eastern and Southern Africa. Khat contains the alkaloid cathinone, a stimulant, which is said to cause excitement, loss of appetite and euphoria.

In Ethiopian Islam, saint veneration is practised by the Sufis. But the Tablīghīs concentrate on Prophet Muḥammad. However, the Tablīghīs do not oppose the practice of saint veneration, unlike the Wahhabis / Salafis.

Spirituality is demonstrated through travelling for faith renewal within the country and abroad for days, weeks and months in the way of Allāh as (*yAllāh musafir*) travellers of Allāh. Everything is spiritual for the Tablīghīs, including eating, sleeping, speaking and participating in a meeting / gathering. Everything has its own etiquette and must be conducted accordingly.

Solidarity is maintained by undertaking religious duties and responsibilities in the spirit of togetherness by organising all the necessary resources, mainly from the participants themselves and, of course, with other people committed to the movement. Those who cannot perform the trips spanning multiple days are encouraged to support others financially. In the Tablīghīs' world, everything is secret and sacred. Documentation and the recording of the events is hardly ever performed.

In Ethiopia, politics is interwoven with religious and ethnic identity. Other Muslims, mainly the Wahhabis / Salafis, encourage engagement with politics but the Ethiopian Tablīghīs, as a group, distance themselves from politics, leaving the issues to Allāh. However, there are some well-educated people who are involved in politics on an individual basis.

In Pakistan, the Tablīghī Jamā'at did not take on a political role until Pakistan became a separate state in 1947. Now, it has a well-defined political agenda which provides ideological and cultural nurture to many hardline religious groups.

One scholar at the School of Oriental and African Studies in London said "there would have been no Taliban without the organisations like the Tablighi Jamaat which create a cultural environment that fosters militant Islamists like the Taliban," further commenting that "Since the 1980s, the Pakistani state has been investing in creating a jihadist infrastructure. It is not only backing armed groups like Lashakar-e-Taiba but also their ideological patrons like the Tablighi Jamaat."

Conclusion

Ethiopia is a house for both Islam and Christianity and has accommodated different religious expressions from both religions for centuries. Tablīghī Jama'at is one such religious expression under Islam which is currently expanding in Ethiopia as a new religious movement within Sunni Islam, though sometimes seen as a sect by the Wahhabis/Salafis and, at times, as an extension of Sufi practices. The Tablīghīs consider themselves as part of Sunni Islam, not as a sect or a new religious movement. However, the way the Tablīghī Jama'at movement operates suggests that they should be considered as a new religious movement within the broader spectrum of Sunni Islam.

The motivation for the Tablīghīs is to strengthen and preserve their Islamic faith and spirituality by extending out from their own vicinity to other places near and far to deliver the call, "Oh Muslims, become Muslims!" which is the motto of the movement. The Ethiopian Tablīghīs have strong operative machinery which includes council (*mashūra*) at all levels with clear and loose structural connectivity: family–local–global.

There is no observed divergence from the normative image of faith renewal and a call to Islam (*da'wa*) of the 'Travellers in Faith' which could hint at the name 'Stealthy Legion' within the Tablīghī Jama'at movement. No violence or political involvement was observed by the author, except the deep longing of the movement seeking the supremacy of Islam throughout the world by fixing their eyes on the world map hung on the wall at the Tablīghī headquarters (*markazes*). The Tablīghīs express their desire by prayer, consultation and mission.

The significant role of the Gurāgēs in the rise and development of the Tablīghī Jama'at movement had been immense, demonstrated through their activities in leadership from local to national level.

Tablīghī spirituality, solidarity and secretiveness are expressed in their life and mission. On the one hand, Tablīghī spirituality and commitment are praised. However, neglecting family responsibilities has been criticised by non-Tablīghīs and non-Muslims. The Tablīghī solidarity and commitment form an amazing experience, demonstrated in social affairs, spiritual duties, participation in *da'wa* tours and by helping others financially. Culturally, the Gurāgēs are known for solidarity, which helps the Tablīghīs to extend such practices as part of the Tablīghī Jama'at movement identity. The missional aspect of the Tablīghī Jama'at movement would be a lesson for anyone who wants to accomplish a task within the community where he or she resides. Tablīghīs' humble beginnings helped the movement to grow and the Gurāgēs are a good illustration in this regard. One can learn how to accomplish missional movement in a particular community from their example.

The Tablīghī Jamā'at accommodates itself within Sunni Islam, theoretically free from debates and avoiding religious and doctrinal arguments but in the Ethiopian case, this is not always possible. On the one hand, Tablīghīs are facing serious opposition from the Wahhabis due to indigenous traditions including chewing *khat*, visiting tombs and saint veneration, yet on the other hand, they receive support and commendation from the Sufis.

The motto of the movement remains simple and clear as Sheikh Ilyas, the founder, coined it: "*Aye Musalmano! Muslamian bano*" (Hindi/Urdu) "*Oh Muslims! Become Muslims.*" Although the objective of the movement is clear and straightforward, it is facing serious challenges from other Sunni movements, particularly the Salafis and Wahhabis who consider it as a cult, due to the six virtues/principles of Tablīghī Jamā'at and other practices which are not welcomed by the Wahhabism/Salafism groups.

So far, there has not been a single case of violence related to the Tablīghī Jamā'at movement in Ethiopia. However, debates and sometimes serious conflicts are taking place among Sunni Islam brothers.

The tolerance level that Tablīghīs have with Sufis encourages them to expand their movement. As part of the faith renewal movements within Islam, they can be located as reformers who work hard to bring faith renewal through humble and low-profile approaches. They maintain their spirituality by travelling far from their own vicinities and practising various Islamic religious duties, helping them to be more spiritual.

The secretiveness of the Ethiopian Tablīghī Jama'at movement is not a surprise, as they want to hide everything and prefer to keep a low profile. Though they are viewed as 'Travellers in Faith' by most scholars in the field, the secretiveness of the movement creates reasonable concern among a minority of scholars.

The Tablīghī Jama'at movement is viewed by a minority as 'Stealthy Legions.' The assumption by some observers that participation in the peaceful *jihad* of Tablīghī Jama'at represents the first stage towards militant jihad or serves as a cover for terrorists has not been demonstrated. This is borne out by evidence that the Tablīghī Jama'at in Ethiopia is a peaceful movement for faith renewal, apart from its political involvement as an organisation, and it has been praised as being peaceful by the past two governments of Ethiopia – the Military Junta (*Derg*) and Ethiopian People's Revolutionary Democratic Front.

Other missionary movements could learn from the Tablīghī Jamā'at, which is approaching its 100-year global existence and over 60 years in Ethiopia. To learn from the Tablīghīs demands humility. To accomplish any missional purpose requires high-level commitment demonstrated by tangible spirituality and solidarity such as that of the Tablīghīs. The Tablīghī Jamā'at movement is self-inspired, self-supported, self-organised and self-governed. Learning from this model will help other organisations in their survival as a missional movement, whether religious or non-religious.